BELIEVING

Understanding the Creed

by
Gerald O'Collins, S.J. and Mary Venturini

PAULIST PRESS
New York/Mahwah, N.J.

Library of Congress Cataloging-in-Publication Data

O'Collins, Gerald.
    Believing: understanding the creed/by Gerald O'Collins and Mary Venturini.
        p. cm.
    Includes bibliographical references.
    ISBN 0-8091-3282-6
    1. Apostles' Creed. I. Venturini, Mary, 1946–   . II. Title.
BT993.2.O27   1991
238'.11—dc20   91-23523
                                                                              CIP

Published by Paulist Press
997 Macarthur Boulevard
Mahwah, NJ 07430

Printed and bound in the
United States of America

Contents

Introduction 1

1. The Human Person 7

2. "I Believe" 16

3. "I Believe in God, the Father Almighty" 25

4. "Creator of Heaven and Earth" 37

5. "Jesus Christ, His Only Son, Our Lord" 48

6. "He Was Conceived by the Power of the Holy Spirit" 57

7. "Born of the Virgin Mary" 66

8. "Suffered Under Pontius Pilate" 76

9. "Crucified, Died and Was Buried" 84

10. "He Descended to the Dead" 93

11. "On the Third Day He Rose Again" 102

12. "He Ascended into Heaven" 113

13. "He Will Come Again To Judge the Living and the Dead" 121

14. "I Believe in the Holy Spirit" 130

15. "The Holy, Catholic Church" 139

16. "The Communion of Saints" 147

17. "The Forgiveness of Sins" 154

18. "The Resurrection of the Body" 162

19. "And Life Everlasting" 172

20. "Amen" 176

Suggestions for Further Reading 177

The Apostles' Creed 178

Introduction

Even if it does not go back to the core group among Jesus' original followers, from the second century the Apostles' Creed established itself as a classic summary of Christian faith. It confesses the basic truths about the God made known to us through the story of the Old and New Testament.

This book will from time to time cite or refer to scriptural texts. But my aim is not to examine the biblical background and roots of the Apostles' Creed. Nor am I concerned to show how the Creed was used and interpreted during twenty centuries of Christianity. Rather I want to reflect on what the various articles contain and mean today. There is a treasure here that is both new and old (Mt 13:52).

The creedal truths portray a surprising God and a God of surprises. In the Apostles' Creed we meet the God of the "new creation" (2 Cor 5:17) whose being and promises invite us to hope for things beyond our wildest dreams. Nevertheless, these new truths also find an echo in the common, "old" experience of human beings. As I wish to argue, the creedal articles attach themselves repeatedly to things we all live and feel and glimpse. The way these articles consistently chime in with our common experience is *also* a reason for finding them to be believable. To prepare the ground for this line of argument, the book begins with two chapters about the human condition and human faith.

Right at the start it seems useful to mention two issues over which many people are genuinely confused. First the Creed confesses a number of truths about God and human beings. It is responding in faith to what God has revealed (Mt 11:25–27; Jn 1:14–18; Heb 1:1). At the same time, both God and human beings remain mysterious and in no way fully understood by the believer. God is a hidden God. What we do not grasp about God far exceeds what we profess to know about God. Our own deepest nature and destiny, if known in part, is not yet fully grasped. Hence the truth and light to which the Creed bears witness leave intact the two corresponding mysteries: the greater mystery of God and the lesser mystery of the human person. What we do not understand goes far beyond what we know through our experience of faith.

The second misconception concerns freedom. Talking about the Creed can conjure up the old delusion that the Christian faith and its truths threaten human freedom. Will believing in the God presented by the Creed leave us no longer free to think and act for ourselves? The biblical tradition would say quite the opposite. God is defined as the God who brings the chosen people home from captivity and exile. Ultimately, God is known as the God who will raise the dead and make all things new (Rev 21:1–5). The truth about God and human beings will set us free. Nowadays it may be easier, even for non-believers, to appreciate that Christian faith makes us free to think and act for ourselves. The alternative, at least for millions of people in Europe, North America and elsewhere, is to let themselves be enslaved by the shallow values of the consumer society and live in the fantasy world of soap operas. For those who refuse to swallow the opium of the people, consumer goods of all kinds, faith offers a liberating, counter-cultural choice. Wherever one lives and whatever problems one faces, at the end of the twentieth century Christian faith remains in essence what it has always been: a call to real freedom, not a lapse into slavery.

I want to express my deep thanks to Mary Venturini for joining me in this project. As journalist, wife and mother of three glorious children, she brings much to an understanding and living of our basic faith. Right from this introduction on, she will comment on and add to what I have written. It was Mary's choice to do that—rather than simply split with me the writing of the chapters by taking half of them.

With love and gratitude I dedicate my share of this book to Karl Holzbauer, S.J. and Joe Übelmesser, S.J.

Gerald O'Collins, S.J.

To walk from our apartment in the center of Rome to the Gregorian University takes about ten minutes. To cover the same journey by car may take half an hour. If you walk you can choose any of a number of ways. You may decide to pass in front of the mighty Roman Pantheon and the church of St Ignatius. Perhaps you will go through the basilica of Santa Maria sopra Minerva which houses the Michelangelo statue of the risen Christ mentioned in Chapter 12. Maybe you will cross the steps of Italy's Chamber of Deputies and the Cabinet Office, or wind up the narrow back streets to the massive baroque monument of the Trevi Fountain. The final destination is the same but what a choice there is along the way!

Go instead by car and you miss all this and much more. Your freedom to choose your road and pick your pace has gone. Instead you must follow the traffic, make a long detour and waste time on the way. Rome, this vital center of our Christian faith, was not built for the car, that everyday reminder of our consumer age.

The Eternal City does not offer those quick and easy answers longed for by contemporary society. The unsuspecting traveler, entranced at first by the city's beauty, suddenly finds that all is not as simple as it seems. Perhaps he grows resentful and faint-hearted. But with a certain perseverance, no little courage and a questioning mind, the real Rome, like the faith at its core, will offer up its momentous secrets.

After many years in Rome I have become accustomed to the city's winding and mysterious ways. Perhaps for this reason I knew when I set off at the start of this book that I would have to end where readers will begin. To have written the introduction first would have been as futile as drawing a map before setting off on a voyage of discovery. Like a fifteenth century explorer I may have known where I wanted to go but I was not sure how I would get there.

Now that I have reached my destination I know that many roads have been left untraveled, distant mountains only dimly glimpsed and fast-running rivers left uncrossed. Above all there is the certainty of many other journeys ahead. But during the eighteen months in which we have explored the Apostles' Creed we have sketched out the map of our Christian belief, based on our discoveries along the way.

Sometimes the going has been hazardous, sometimes easy. It has always been exciting. Occasionally it has been lonely, but it has never been lived alone. The journey has been made possible because it has built on the experience of the many who have gone before us, and its purpose has been to leave an account for those who come after. And while we have worked individually, not discussing our ideas before setting them down on paper, nor modifying them after, except to make minor corrections, we have always had a sense of working in dialogue.

It seemed important from the start that we should share each chapter. Had we divided the book between us, one would have cut the other out from key tenets of our belief. To have written about the creation and not the virgin birth, to have taken the chapter on the crucifixion without being able to reflect on the resurrection would have done violence to our faith as a whole.

4

Our faith is above all a whole, not bits and pieces to be selected at will. We were perhaps tempted to skip the sections of the Creed which touch on the subjects of hell or the last judgment as not applicable to our faith today. But we resisted the temptation, and I certainly have found that the struggle to give meaning to these difficult concepts has lent greater value to my journey through the Creed.

More than this it seemed necessary to share, not divide, this book because our belief is not lived out in isolation but in communion. Our Christian faith involves a living dialogue. Our relationship with God and our fellows stagnates, atrophies and may finally die unless we make a constant effort to communicate with others. Here in these pages we have shared the experiences of our belief, in an attempt to leave signposts along our way for those who choose to make a similar voyage of discovery.

I should like to thank Father Gerald for asking me to share this book with him. Working together has been a rare privilege and a great inspiration for which I shall always be grateful.

I dedicate my part in this common experience to all my family with my love and thanks, knowing that each one of them has made these pages possible in a very special way.

Mary Venturini
Rome
7 February 1990

1

The Human Person

W ho are we? How should we best describe our
common humanity? What is the ultimate nature and destiny of human beings? How can we most appropriately sum up what we human beings are and are to
become?

If you look for a clean, uncluttered answer, you will
find that a good number are available. For many centuries
it was customary to talk of human beings as "rational animals." Then along came Charles Darwin (1809–82) to de-
velop the theory that we evolved from lower forms of life.
Darwin's answer presented *homo evolvens* or evolutionary
man. By challenging his public to reform radically an unjust society, Karl Marx (1818–83) left us with a picture of
human beings as creative masters of themselves and their
world (*homo faber*). Marx's grave in London carries the
message: "The philosophers have only interpreted the
world in various ways. The point however is to change it!"

A third great moulder of modern views about our existence, Sigmund Freud (1856–1939), explored at depth
human psychology and the role of unconscious forces in
shaping our behavior. *Homo psychologicus* or "psychological man" could serve as a tag for Freud's version of our
human condition.

When the theories of Darwin, Marx and Freud burst
on the scene, many Christians found themselves extremely disconcerted. Some of their criticisms were

7

wrongheaded. Yet they had every right to reject the anti-God elements in the interpretations of Marx, Freud and Darwin (or, more accurately, Darwin's disciples), as well as other unsatisfactory items in the thought of all three writers. At the same time, Darwin, Marx and Freud have enriched our grasp of human life and its problems. I will speak later about Darwinism—in the chapter on creation. Marx was not utterly wrong in observing the importance of economic factors, rightly protested against massive social evils, and encouraged us to test the truth of theories also in practice—by noting what a given theory about the human condition leads its supporters to do or leave undone.

Thus far I have pointed to three of the most striking and influential modern accounts of our common humanity. I could press on to list and summarize what Soren Kierkegaard (1813–55), Friedrich Wilhelm Nietzsche (1844–1900), existentialists like Jean-Paul Sartre (1905–1980), Martin Heidegger (1889–1976) or Gabriel Marcel (1889–1973), sociologists since Emile Durkheim (1858–1917) and experts in the other human sciences have to tell us about our common nature and situation. One might hope that if we heard all the answers, eventually everything would fall into place and we would have a well-rounded version of our present condition and future prospects.

At this point, however, I prefer to come clean and sketch what I find to be the best way of talking about our nature and destiny. Last summer in the German city of Nuremberg a modern bronze statue of Job helped to focus my reflection. Naked and hunched up, he sits near the door of a late Gothic church and alongside the main street that cuts across the city from the railway station. Handsome, well-fed people moved briskly past Job on their way to the sales in those temples of consumer society, the huge department stores.

Foreign and local tourists came off the intercity trains

8

to see the paintings of Albrecht Dürer and the late-medieval sculptures that make Nuremberg an artistic Mecca. Other people hurried by to get their tickets for *the* musical event of the year, Placido Domingo's outdoor concert that was to fill the old marketplace. I turned away from the busy street to look at Job and think about my question: Who are we?

His gaunt shoulders show how pain has got the better of him. Yet something about his face slips beyond mere resignation to hint at real human hope. The thought came to me: "Job expresses the truth of our common humanity. Each one of us suffers (*homo dolens*) and hopes (*homo sperans*). We are all beings who suffer and hope—the shoppers, the tourists and the concert-goers, no less than the lonely soldiers and derelicts who drift around the railway station."

What I want to do now is unpack the sufferings and hopes that can offer a well-documented account of our human condition. First, the sufferings. We can name the three forces that produce our sufferings: death, meaninglessness and hatred.

As much or more than many thinkers before him, Heidegger stressed the notion of our human existence as "being-toward-death." We all live under the shadow of death. Biologically speaking, none of us has a future. At the same time, the figure of Job reminds us that death also expresses itself in forms other than biological extinction. Death is not simply the knob at the end of the walking-stick of life. It invades the whole of our existence. Job lost his children, his possessions, his health and his good name. Deadly forces stripped him naked. In less dramatic ways death is constantly robbing everyone. Friendships break up, chances are missed and time runs away from us all.

Granted the losses that haunt every life's journey, it is literal death and the fear of it that cast their painful shadow over the whole human race. Each year famine and contaminated water take the lives of millions of children

9

and adults. Fighting ends in Vietnam only to erupt in Afghanistan, Cambodia, Iraq, Iran, Lebanon, Nicaragua, and other crucified parts of our world. Officially Colombia may not be in a state of war, but the paramilitary forces, guerillas, drug barons and others see to it that over three hundred people die violently every month. Despite some healthy moves on the part of the Americans and the Russians, thousands of atomic missiles still threaten the existence of humanity. In any case the deterioration of the ozone layer may see us all die through radiation and genetic changes.

In its many forms death brings pain to human beings. We suffer death or inflict it on ourselves and others. The dramatic story of Job reminds us of the second great source of suffering: the mysterious meaninglessness that can envelop our lives and paralyze our activity. Why should an innocent and good man like Job suffer the way he did? The apparent absurdity of our world and our personal existence can bring some people to a standstill. Why should vast sums of money be squandered on sophisticated military weapons when a tiny fraction of that money could wipe out leprosy in our world? What is the point and purpose of my life? A sense of hollow, desperate emptiness drives many people today toward drug addiction and self-destruction.

After I looked at Job in Nuremberg, I went across the city to say mass in an old people's home. Over breakfast the matron told me of her two years in a Russian prisoner-of-war camp. "It was a very hard time, but I learned much from that experience." She paused and then went on: "What still seems utterly meaningless, though, was the death of my twelve year old brother. Soldiers beat him to death."

Like Job, every human being can tell the story of the isolation, misunderstanding and even hatred that he or she has experienced. The effects of that third source of suffering are writ large in the story of many groups in our modern world: Afghans, Cambodians, Guatemalans, Indians, Palestinians, South African blacks and millions of refugees driven from their homeland by hatred and cruel indifference.

One Sunday in Nuremberg I took part in a silent march to the place where fifty years before the first of the city's two synagogues was torn down. Twenty or thirty Jews stood in front of the monument and their cantor sang a psalm of lamentation in memory of the millions of his brothers and sisters systematically wiped out by hatred.

The Jewish people, Job, that matron in Nuremberg and many other cases write large the three major negative forces that shape our existence: death, meaninglessness, and hatred or callous indifference.

Human beings suffer but they also hope to find life, meaning and love. In fact, we all experience situations when we feel ourselves deeply alive. New life can be given to us when something seemed to threaten our whole existence. Or else the light dawns and we see some meaning in a puzzling or even absurd situation. Things fall into place and we enjoy a fresh direction and purpose. In our century no one has stressed more our search for meaning than the Viennese psychologist Viktor Frankl (b.1905).

Imprisoned in a concentration camp, he found meaning given him through his human and religious experiences. That allowed him to survive and even live in a richer way, whereas other prisoners for whom the whole situation was totally absurd simply lay down and died.

Third, there is the gift of love that comes to us from our relatives, from extra-special friends and—sometimes and most wonderful of all—from strangers who act toward us with real love simply because we need their help and we share their common humanity. Love does make the world go round. Those unfortunates who truly fail to experience friendship and love are doomed to live less than properly human lives. But, at least from time to time, the overwhelming majority of people experience the power of love and friendship—through their marriage, their family, their friends and their place of work. The sense of loving and being loved is the breath that gives life to our human condition.

Like Job we all suffer. But we also seek and experience life, meaning and love. I cannot think of any better way of describing and (partially) explaining happiness as those times we feel deeply the gift of life, the meaningfulness of things and the joy of love. The truly happy moments come through those experiences of living, understanding and loving.

Our problem is that we experience life, meaning and love in fragmentary, incomplete and temporary ways. Like Faust in Goethe's great work we want the moment of happiness to continue forever: "Do stay on; you are so beautiful (*verweile doch, du bist so schön*)." The partial experience of happiness fuels our existence. We forge ahead, hoping and yearning for full life, complete understanding and total love.

This is the best way I know of presenting our common human existence. With Job we suffer from death, absurdity and isolation or even hatred. Like the Job I studied in Nuremberg we look for life, meaning and love. We may go looking for them in the wrong way or in the wrong places. Nevertheless, our human nature itself sends us on the constant search for life, meaning and love. Are they ever to be found in their fullness? If so, where and how? Those are the fundamental questions our human condition puts to us.

Before reflecting on the answer the Christian Creed proposes, we need to examine a second basic factor, human faith. After all this book addresses the way the faith of a human being can become the belief of a Christian. I have offered a vision of the human condition. We will turn to its necessary concomitant, faith.

At approximately the same time as you, Gerald, were contemplating the man-made statue of Job in a busy Nuremberg street, across the other side of Europe I was gazing down at the granite cliffs which run along the north coast of the tiny island where I grew up. They drop steeply several hundred feet to the sea. Every now and then the hard face gives way to gorse, heather and bracken, and here more often than not there is a trace of a path winding down to the shore. Occasionally you can see a small human speck move along this thread in search of the sea.

Once, long ago, each parish in the island had a sanctuary path leading from its church to the coast, along which the hunted could escape from injustice and persecution. It was the Almighty's gift of freedom to all those who sought for help, a freedom that was not without its risks, as the waters around the island are treacherous, claiming lives each year. Man, who has been gazing down from these cliffs since pre-historic times, is still a victim of the currents and the winds, perhaps now even more than in the past.

When I grew up, there was a lore of the tides and the seasons. Certain dangers were known and avoided. Few boats were moored along the coast and then only in the traditionally protected anchorages. Today every cove, safe haven or not, is filled with luxury craft, the symbols of the consumer society. And inexperienced sailors venture out in the hopes that their powerful engines will get them through danger or that, if all else fails, the ever-vigilant lifeboat will come to their rescue. Sometimes they are unlucky. Their modern technology breaks down and help arrives too late.

In this first chapter you ask a question which we constantly raise as thinking and feeling human beings: Who are we and how can we best describe our nature? You have contemplated the genius of man in the art of the master craftsman. You have picked great figures of nineteenth century thought, Darwin, Marx, Freud and others, to illustrate your arguments. I have chosen the human speck along the sanctuary path in search of a perilous freedom, the prey of the elements, a victim of Darwin's natural selection, Marx's economic exploitation, and the deep subconscious emotions discovered by Freud. You have selected the conditions of suffering and hope to describe the human condition. I would choose two other characteristics—doubt and confidence: doubt for the small speck faced with the countless dangers of the modern world and confidence in the ability of man as reflected in his master works of genius.

If I were to choose an artistic representation of an Old Testament figure to sum up the human condition I should pick Michelangelo's David, the young man from Bethlehem sent out to battle against the odds, the shepherd become king, the sinner, the adulterer, the murderer, but a man chosen by God. In that larger-than-life statue the powerful body expresses the immense confidence of man. But look at David's face and you see the doubt of all humans contained in the shadow of his frown.

So we have suffering tempered by hope in the figure of Job and confidence mixed with doubt in the statue of David. Isn't it perhaps this permanent conflict of opposites which is at the heart of the human condition? Man seems small, insignificant and in the grip of powerful natural forces and disasters, but is also capable of conquering oceans in elementary sailing boats guided only by the stars, of scaling ice-covered mountains with rudimentary equipment, of deciphering the infinity of space or the microscopic codes of the living cell. Human beings may be driven by suppressed emotions but they are still capable of rational thought. Freud after all was groping after a rational explanation for seemingly irrational behavior. Humans may be conditioned by social forces but quite often they step out of line to protest. They are creative and loving but are also full of hate and destruction. At the very moment they are living they are also dying.

It is perhaps at times closest to death that we most value life. It is in moments of hate that we long for love. It is in periods of disorder and confusion that we search for order and meaning.

While recognizing a state of conflict as characteristic of the human condition, most of us look for a way out. It is in this search for an end to all conflict and doubt that men and women, restless explorers of the unknown, reach for God.

It was in fact during a particularly confusing time in the life of the early church that the Apostles' Creed was formulated. For the first hundred years or more after the death of Christ, there was no such summary of Christian belief. It was almost as though those early followers of Christ *knew* what it was to be a Christian. Their belief was too certain and obvious for them to have to state it. It was only as doubts, conflicts and uncertainties crept in that it became necessary to formalize belief, to put up barriers against certain mistaken interpretations and heresies.

Even today, as we stand to say the Creed, we are defining what we believe and confronting it with what we do not. How many Christians, in that awesome moment of reciting their belief, have not asked themselves at some time or another, like James Joyce in *Portrait of an Artist as a Young Man:* Is this what I really believe? There, on this frontier between Christian belief and non-belief, the Creed stands its guard. Some like Joyce will find that once the questioning sets in they will never be able to say the Creed again, or certainly not with their previous childlike trust. Others in their moment of doubt will go on to greater faith and conviction.

2

"I Believe"

Faith is a necessary and inevitable component of human life. I find it extremely difficult, if not impossible, to imagine a man or woman who showed no signs of any faith whatsoever.

Let me explain what I mean by using the three famous questions with which Immanuel Kant (1724–1804) summarized the whole thrust of his intellectual endeavors: "What can I know? What ought I to do? What may I hope for?" Whether they ever articulate it fully or not, all human beings answer these questions in a way that shapes and organizes their lives. They take a stand about their knowledge of themselves, other human beings, the rest of the world and God. They have some story to tell about the ultimate truth of things. Likewise they all have something to say about the values and ideals according to which they ought to live. Third, even if they do not accept an after-life, they will have some account to offer about what they may hope for from the future.

Admittedly people may find it hard to define clearly their belief. They may only vaguely accept the existence of a divine being and our life beyond death. Or they may profess to be skeptical about God and a personal after-life. Nevertheless, all people will state something in answer to the question: What can we know about the ultimate nature of things (= their confession)? They will likewise have something to say about basic values, duties and ideals

16

(= their real or alleged commitment). They will also, however tentatively, point to the deepest hopes that keep them going (= their confidence for the future).

Their faith defines people and groups of people: as Buddhists, Christians, Hindus, Jews, humanists, Marxists, Muslims and so forth. I think it reasonable to use the word "faith" in all these cases. Like the religious believers, Marxists and atheistic humanists will describe and explain for us their confession, their commitment and their confidence for the future. Like their religious counterparts they hold their beliefs through what they have experienced, read or been told by others. For them, too, "faith" comes from what is heard—to adapt St. Paul's classic teaching (Rom 10:17).

I want to argue that in all cases, in religious as in non-religious systems, faith is free. Some psychologists and others would beg to disagree. We are not really free in our systems of belief. Experiences in early childhood or massive social pressures have simply programmed us to accept a certain confession, to endorse some values and entertain some particular hopes for the future. I certainly do not wish to dismiss lightly the position of those who claim we are totally determined by forces beyond our control. Yet I have always noticed that at least three points strongly call into question that view. First, one can object that those who hold the view have themselves been simply socially conditioned to hold their position and hence are no more convincing than anyone else. Or are they claiming a quite special enlightenment for themselves? The truth has set them free, they have moved beyond the bounds of any faith, and can pronounce freely and truthfully about the enslaved condition of the rest of us. Second, a thoroughgoing denial of human freedom has a massive language-problem on its hands. Many words that we commonly use presuppose the fact that human beings are free and responsible. Think of terms like gratitude, praise, pride, blame, indignation, resentment and shame. Those who deny real

17

freedom will either have to purge these words from our common vocabulary or else reinterpret them in a peculiar manner that does not correspond to common usage. Either way a complete denial of human freedom has an extraordinary language-problem to cope with. Third, there is an area in which the legal experts are the final judges. Yet something can be said from a common sense point of view. The genuinely free responsibility of adult human beings appears to be an indispensable element in our law and its working. If freedom is denied in the case of religious beliefs and practices, it should also be denied in the area of public law. But the consequences of denying legal freedom would be extraordinarily alarming and not too distinguishable from the society George Orwell presented in *1984*.

In the case of all religions and other systems of belief faith is free or it is not truly there at all. This is not to ignore the fact that our decision to believe and all our actions are in part determined and conditioned by forces beyond our control. Nevertheless, on some occasions and to some degree we can freely and responsibly act. We can believe and live out our faith or else freely fail to live out the faith we profess.

In the first chapter I mentioned a silent march in August 1988 to the place in Nuremberg where fifty years earlier the Nazis had destroyed the city's chief synagogue. A monument was unveiled, a Jewish cantor sang, the present head of the Jewish community in Nuremberg prayed. There was a prayer too from the leading Protestant pastor of the city, a prayer which never explicitly mentioned faith or freedom but which would be unintelligible without those two elements. I quote his words in full:

Lord, our God, full of shame we think of what happened here fifty years ago and we pray to you. Fill us all with your Spirit, so that finally we recognize in one another our brothers and sisters, so that—with all prej-

18

udices overcome—love instead of hate may rule the hearts of human beings and peace may bind us all together. Grant that in our city and land people may never again be persecuted and their places of worship destroyed. Lead us into a future in which each person helps and takes responsibility for the other and in which each person is there on hand for the other, just as you, our God, are there on hand for us all.

This moving prayer not only presupposed throughout the freedom of faith but also spoke of another utterly essential element in faith: God's grace, or, in more personal terms, the guiding influence of the Holy Spirit. But before taking up this theme in the context of Christian faith, I would like to add one further thought about the common ground between Christian faith and all other forms of human faith.

To some extent all systems of faith are, strictly speaking, unprovable and go beyond the evidence. On the one hand, it is difficult or even impossible to imagine a faith that would dispense itself one hundred percent from reason and be simply a wild leap into total darkness. All systems of belief have at least some signs, reasons and evidence that they point to, even if admittedly some travel on a road between reality and sheer fantasy. On the other hand, however, the Christian creed itself is not completely provable. If it were, it would simply become a set of scientifically demonstrable conclusions and not a faith by which one can freely live.

Thus far this chapter has claimed that human beings are by their very nature believers. It has been suggested that faith always involves some confession, commitment and confidence for the future, that faith "comes from hearing," and yet is always at least partly free in going beyond the hard evidence.

To introduce the rest of this book, let me add some specific items about Christian faith. First, unlike Hinduism, Marxism and many other faiths, Christianity is utterly focused on an historical person, Jesus of Nazareth. In their worship Christians constantly remember and celebrate the events of Jesus' birth, life, death and resurrection. Second, while the Christian faith certainly invites men and women to accept and experience something new, it takes up and illuminates our deepest human experiences. It is this extraordinary blend of the new and the old that constantly intrigues me about Christian faith. On the one hand, this faith makes staggeringly new claims such as the salvation of all people coming through an utterly disgraceful and humiliating death on the cross. On the other hand, in an astonishing way it illuminates the basic human quest for life, meaning and love and our flight from their negative counterparts (death, meaninglessness and hatred). The chapters that follow will have to substantiate what it is about fundamental human experience that blends the new and the old.

A third "item" that is specifically important for Christian faith is the role of the Holy Spirit. From the outset Christians were convinced that their faith came not only from hearing the good news about Jesus Christ but also through the invisible, yet real help of God's Spirit. Our chapter on the Holy Spirit will seek to elucidate that conviction.

After these two opening chapters on the human condition and the nature of faith, we explore one by one the articles of faith. That will mean concentrating somewhat on the confessional dimension. Nevertheless, it is not possible to explain at any depth what we profess as Christians while saying nothing about our commitment and our confident hope for the future. After all the Apostles' Creed begins by declaring "I believe in God" and does not simply state "I believe that God exists." Right from the outset the Creed goes beyond a mere confession of faith.

Of the three elements that make up Christian faith, the hard challenge comes from the second. It is perfectly possible to profess verbally the Creed but practice the faith only when we feel the need to do so. Prayer and worship can become sporadic. In a destructive and self-destructive fashion, current desires and resentments can control the decisions taken when moral crises occur in our lives. The real commitment of faith is much more than a good feeling about Christianity that is occasionally prodded into activity by some vague or urgent need. As we know, no marriage is likely to survive, let alone produce deep and lasting happiness on the basis of such a superficial commitment. Christians have followed their Jewish antecedents in describing faith precisely as involving a steadfast and loving covenant or marriage bond between God and believers. Like marriage and similar deep human commitments, Christian faith calls on its adherents to have the freedom and courage to be persistently loyal. It invites us to find the point and purpose of our existence through a lived faith in God who is Father, Son and Holy Spirit.

C hristian faith reaches out beyond reason and it is more than hope. It is a free choice that we make at some stage during our lives as Christians, whether earlier because we have been brought up in a Christian family, or later because we have been converted from other religious or humanistic beliefs. In this chapter you tackle the question of freedom head-on. I was therefore all the more surprised that you did not mention the question of choice. It is when we confront a choice that our commitment and faith as Christians is really put to the test.

The ability to make a choice is one of the hardest things to teach a child. How often my children have said, "Mummy, what should I do? Can't you decide for me?" When they were small I tended not to confuse them with too much choice. It caused anxiety, uncertainty and a feeling of insecurity. They were not capable of coming to a decision, and needed help and reassurance. Gradually as they moved out of a babyhood into childhood and then on into adolescence, it became essential as part of their growth toward maturity that they should learn to choose between alternative courses of action and ways of behavior. While I still point to important factors which they should take into consideration when making a choice, there are times when I know that the decision—whether about school work, leisure or personal friendships—must be theirs and not mine if it is to be of value.

Even as adults there are crucial moments in our lives when we find it difficult to choose between different courses of action. We turn here and there asking for advice and longing for someone else to shoulder our responsibility. It was at such a moment that Pontius Pilate held the life of Christ in his hands. He is probably history's most extreme case of a man who came down in favor of political expediency rather than moral justice and then passed his responsibility on down the line. But his was not an uncommon dilemma. Many men and women in positions of power, whether economic or political, take this same road day after day.

As you point out in the last paragraph, we may confess our faith but never make much of an active commitment. Those of us who have been brought up in a society based on Christian morality may wait for years before having to make a choice. We shall go along with the accepted forms and practices of our surrounding culture. It may be quite a long time before we are asked to step out of line to defend our Christian beliefs. It is only when we are faced with the alternative of taking the safe road or the dangerous cliff path that the full implication of our freedom suddenly becomes apparent.

That we do have a freedom of choice is evident in the lives of countless Christians, from the apostles onward, who have had the courage to go against the conventions of their times. To exercise this freedom may mean loneliness, rejection and persecution. In the most extreme cases we may demonstrate our freedom by rejecting an easy conformity in favor of a choice which leads us to death. At the heart of the Christian freedom therefore lies the paradox of our faith: we choose a way of life that may lead us to a cruel and lonely death. There could be few more compelling signs of our freedom than this.

Our Christian faith, however, need not be either dramatic or spectacular. It may spring instead from the ordinary moments of everyday life and it often does. We all love the great figures of our faith. We long to follow the charismatic leaders, the martyrs and the saints. We yearn for the irrefutable miracle and the really spectacular conversion.

However, faith may be put to its hardest test in the very ordinariness of daily existence. Faith often comes quite easily in moments of great tension, suffering, sorrow and drama. It is more difficult to nourish and discern in the humdrum moments of our lives. Closeness to the Almighty is felt much more easily listening to music in the quiet of a magnificent church than in the jostle of a hot and crowded bus.

I should like to end this chapter with one of my favorite stories about faith which I heard one evening in a busy Rome restaurant on an occasion when religion was far from any of our minds. Italians are wonderful story-tellers and have a marvelous capacity to poke fun at themselves while hitting an inner core of truth. After a series of up-to-the-minute political jokes I suddenly found myself listening to the following tale.

A poor fisherman put out to sea one day for his catch, but while he was setting his nets a storm blew up, catching him ill-prepared. The boat started to sink and the fisherman who was a religious fellow knelt down to pray for help. As he prayed, a boat came up, circled round him, and one of the men aboard threw our friend a rope. The fisherman ignored the rope and went on praying. The boat circled again but this time the fisherman looked up and shouted across the stormy water: "Don't worry! Everything will be all right. I am a man of great faith and I know that the Lord will save me."

The storm continued, the little boat sank further into the waves, and the fisherman continued to pray. Before long another craft appeared on the horizon, saw the fisherman's distress, and moved in to the rescue. "There's no need of your help," shouted the fisherman once again. "I am a man of great faith and the Lord will protect me." Feeling helpless the men in the second boat also made for safety.

By this time the little fishing vessel had shipped a great deal of water and its owner prayed harder than ever. As the wind reached its height, another boat came along. "No, no," cried the fisherman yet again as the third crew tried to take him aboard. "I have great faith that all will be well and that God will save me."

The third boat soon turned away. Before long the little vessel sank below the waves and the fisherman drowned.

In a reproachful mood our friend reached heaven and asked to see the Lord. "How could you let one of your faithful down so badly," he complained. "I went to church all my life, I prayed, I fasted, I kept all the commandments, I did everything a true Christian should do, but look what happened."

"Well," replied the Lord with a puzzled frown, "I tried my best. I sent three boats to your rescue but you turned them all away."

3

"I Believe in God, the Father Almighty"

O n my last visit to Nuremberg I went on a summer afternoon through one of the medieval gates on the west side of the city, walked under the trees along the River Pegnitz and came to the cemetery of St. John. Albrecht Dürer and other famous Christians are buried there. Many of the old tombs belong to great families of the city and carry messages of warning and hope. One is told, "Keep on the watch, for you know not the day nor the hour," but one also reads: "Blessed are the dead who die in the Lord." Some of the tombs go back to the late middle ages. For most of the year the whole cemetery is ablaze with flowers.

On the left toward the river you find the tomb of Ludwig Feuerbach. The gray stone covering the grave bears his profile in bronze and the dates "Born 1804, died 1872." He had already delivered his message through his writings: the Christian God was nothing else than the projection of human wishes and needs. Men and women should be liberated from this illusion.

Was Feuerbach right? Is the all-powerful, all-knowing, and perfectly good, just and loving God of the Jewish-Christian tradition merely a product of our needs and imagination? Or is there an omnipresent, infinitely caring personal power beyond ourselves who guides our lives and to whom we owe our deepest allegiance?

Millions of people believe in God and have found a thoroughly satisfying life by doing so. But there are also many people who deny or doubt a personal divine being and go about the business of living without faith in God. Obviously belief in God is, to some extent, voluntary and by no means inevitable. Believers cheerfully accept or should so accept this fact. Literally proving their faith in God would be a contradiction in terms. Faith freely goes beyond the evidence or else it cannot claim to be a personal faith in a personal God.

Yet there is evidence that one can point to. There are reasons and signs that can combine to justify belief in God. The year 1990 marks a century since the death of John Henry Newman, who is valued for many things, but not least for his view that in religious (and other) matters evidence works cumulatively. When put together, reasons converge to bring us to the truth.

In some circles, it is axiomatic that our mind alone can settle the issue of God. But this approach strikes me as misguided as claiming that our mind alone can settle the issue of our richest friendships and loves. The God that I believe to exist is not some very distant managing director of the universe, but the uniquely dearest friend that any of us could ever have. The existence and relationship of such a God to us can be properly decided only on the basis of our total human experience. Our freedom, our fears and hopes, our intuitions, our patterns of behavior, the loud thoughts that may come in moments of solitude—in short everything serious that is involved in the whole story of our personal experience—come into play when we raise and settle the question of God.

The French mathematician and philosopher Blaise Pascal (1623–1662) is often remembered for his claim that belief in God was the safest bet. The believer will enter into eternal happiness if he is right or oblivion if he is wrong. The unbeliever must face the daunting alternative of oblivion or damnation. In his *Pensée* (nr 418) Pascal certainly proposed this famous or notorious wager. But what really counted for him personally was the extraordinary experience of God in Jesus Christ which happened to him on the night of November 23, 1654. For the rest of his life he carried on his person an account of that experience. After Pascal's death that account was discovered sewn into his clothing.

The opening chapter of this book interpreted our human existence as a constant search for the fullness of life, meaning and love. Will we find in and through the divine power the fullness of life for which we yearn? Are the things we experience just a succession of pleasant or unpleasant facts? Or through an all-wise and ever-active God will they one day fall into place and make eminently good sense? Will we ever go beyond the fragmentary and imperfect experiences of love that dot our lives to find in someone a complete and utterly satisfying love?

Believers answer these questions affirmatively, and for the most part they do so because they have experienced God in the heart of their being. These depth-experiences of God are closely aligned with prayer and the willingness to pause and let God enter one's heart and mind. It was precisely in terms of falling on his knees to pray that C.S. Lewis described the climax of his own passage to belief. In prayer God comes to seek us out—if we allow that to happen.

Several years ago Gerald Priestland interviewed me during his radio program *The Case Against God.* In his book which has the same title he mentions that while we sat talking, the lights failed and "it gave us a pretty picture of two men talking about God in the dark." What struck me even more was what Priestland suggested after concluding the interview: "Let us wrap our conversation in silence and prayer." I cannot think of any better advice to give anyone who approaches the question of God: "Let your search take you into silence and prayer. See what signs of God's presence that experience brings you."

Feuerbach and his various successors have encouraged us to dispense with the God-hypothesis and get on with building a better human society. For decades secular humanism, Marxism, atheistic schools of psychology, Nietzsche's vision of super-men, and hopes engendered by theories about human evolution exerted an extraordinary grip upon the imaginations and aspirations of millions. But the brave new world has not come. Communism is not the only god that has failed.

Feuerbach's ideas helped to shape Nietzsche who assured us that "the Christian concept of God is sick, corrupt, the contradiction of life." Nietzsche's own ideas flowed into Adolf Hitler's National Socialism, a thoroughly sick, corrupt and life-destructive system if there ever was one.

Freud's psychoanalysis was a monumental achievement. But his greatest disciple, C.G. Jung (1875–1961), moved away from his teacher's atheism. He discovered that the common problem with all his patients above the age of thirty-five was finding a religious attitude to life. It was not religion but its absence that caused neuroses. Beyond question, the evolution of modern research and technology has produced astonishing results in medicine, agriculture, human communications and other fields. But it is trite to remark that those who pinned all their hopes on finding a fuller human life through this material progress have failed to establish a more satisfactory human alternative to a life that finds its sense of direction through faith in God.

In his magisterial *Anthropology in Theological Perspective* (German original, 1985) Wolfhart Pannenberg investigates various human sciences to put his case: any academic discipline that examines human beings at depth will or should raise the question of God. He argues that we cannot fully understand and interpret the nature and destiny of our common humanity without recognizing God. One could rightly add that the history of the twentieth

28

century witnesses in a terrifying fashion to what happens when individuals, groups and whole nations decide to live without God.

Of course, one should not overdo criticisms of godless societies and their results. After all very many atrocities have been committed in God's own name. Nevertheless, the evidence that has so far come in from modern world history hardly suggests that denying God or simply adopting the posture of religious indifference clearly enhances human life by making it more meaningful and loving.

Thus far this chapter has claimed that belief in God is a free choice very much tied up with deep personal experiences and prayer. Believers feel that they are known and loved by someone. They are aware of a divine presence that focuses their life and to which they freely respond with loving trust. Many believers have compared their faith-commitment to the situation of happily married people. Like belief in God, marriage is by no means the easy fulfillment of a romantic dream. Nor can one publicly and scientifically prove the personal experience of a richer life, meaning and love that marriage has brought. Nevertheless, believers like married people can and do bear witness to a relationship which they believe in and to which they have freely responded in love.

The next chapter in this book will, in part, be concerned to justify *intellectually* a belief in God as creator. All the same, merely intellectual arguments for God and the divine existence remain of limited value. I suspect that, often without realizing it, believers have resorted to such arguments as one way of witnessing to and articulating their personal experience of God.

Where then does all that leave my talk about some reasons, signs and evidence for God's existence? It is clearly not enough to criticize the alternative of non-belief and leave it at that. There are signs supporting belief, but they work differently for believers and non-believers (and the doubtful).

From the inside believers experience the way faith keeps life in working order. It provides the vision by which they can live, find meaning, and experience love given and received. The lived truth confirms itself over and over again in practice.

What of the non-believers who by definition do not share from the inside the experience of faith? What evidence is available for them? At the very least they see and hear the witness of believers. From the inside believers testify that faith is supremely worthwhile. Once again the witness of their lives is something like that of happily married couples who testify to their children and other younger people of the next generation that marriage is worth trying. Further, from the outside non-believers can test faith in God by seeing the observable differences in the life of believers. Does faith bring an enviable joy, peace and sense of direction? Does it look like a thoroughly coherent and workable commitment? What does it lead believers to do for others?

Regrettably there is some truth in Nietzsche's gibe against Christ and Christians: "His followers should look more redeemed." However, despite their massive failures to live out fully their faith, Christian believers have been largely out on their own in caring for lepers, the terminally ill and the utterly destitute. In general, for all their defects, Christians have led the way in establishing hospitals, schools and orphanages. Christ's words about feeding the hungry, clothing the naked, visiting prisoners, caring for the sick and welcoming strangers have produced rich and lasting results.

What is widely and rightly regarded as the great challenge to Christian faith and indeed any faith in God is not the behavior of believers but rather the behavior of God. How can one reconcile faith in an all-loving and all-powerful God with suffering, above all the suffering of innocent people? The city where I wrote this chapter raises this question in a striking fashion. Those who come from Nur-

30

emberg's central railway station pass the statue of Job, who expresses for all time the mystery of unmerited human suffering. In utter misery Job cried out against the God at whose hands he suffered cruelly. Beyond the railway tracks one finds Nuremberg's parade grounds where Hitler staged his monster rallies. In the other direction you cross a bridge to reach the monument recalling the destruction of Nuremberg's main synagogue and the suffering of God's chosen people. Even before 1941 dozens of Jews from Nuremberg had been killed. Between 1941 and 1944 over 1,600 other Jews were taken from the city to concentration camps; of these only seventy-two survived. Nuremberg seems an appropriate place to put God on trial over the issue of unmerited human suffering.

Once again those who deny the divine reality do not enjoy any clear advantage over believers when faced with pogroms, wars, massive injustice, cancer, handicapped children and further public and private sufferings without end. For a hundred years or more, non-believers of various kinds have pinned their hopes on *education* and other social programs as the way to reduce the pain for various classes and nations, if not for all human beings. So far from arriving, the brave new world of non-believers seems further away than ever. What can non-believers do now? Try even harder to reduce suffering by reeducating and reconstructing the whole world? Or fall silent over the mystery of evil and simply resign themselves to the absurdity of the human situation?

Christian believers know themselves to have accepted freely God's offer of friendship. But what can they say to a God who permits the atrocities connected with Auschwitz, Beirut, Dresden, Hiroshima, the Katyn Woods and so many other blood-stained places on the face of our earth?

First things first. A tremendous amount of suffering arises from the selfishness, cruelty and indifference of human beings—in short, from the misuse of their God-given

31

freedom. It would be monstrous to argue that having made us free, God should then tinker with our freedom and either bribe or coerce us constantly into behaving decently toward each other. If anyone is to go on trial for causing pain and unmerited suffering on a worldwide scale, the charges should be first brought against the visible perpetrators, human beings.

At the same time, there is still a residue of seemingly unjust pain and suffering that we cannot attribute to human beings. In a word, Job's problem. At the end God speaks to Job out of the whirlwind and leaves the reader not with an answer but with questions. Who are we to criticize God and put God on trial? What does God owe any of us? Radically speaking, we deserve nothing: all is gift. Yet suffering, and especially unmerited suffering, calls for a more personal answer that may not explain the mystery but will at least point the way to what we can do with suffering. That will be one of the aims in the chapters on Christ's suffering and crucifixion.

I have pushed this chapter of yours aside for too long. Now on a dry, rather barren morning, when the untidy remains of a hot summer have not quite given way to the freshness of autumn, I can no longer escape the thoughts your pages have provoked.

I always dread the question of God and suffering because I know I have few convincing answers. "If your God is what you say he is, why does he allow all this suffering in the world?" is a nasty blow I try to duck when I can. It reminds me of those overwhelming feelings of desperation I used to get when as a small child at school the teacher would say in reaction to some misdeed or stupidity of mine, "Well, if your parents have brought you up like this, they can't be much good, can they?"

I loved my parents profoundly and considered that they could do no wrong. It was therefore more than I could bear that my shortcomings should be blamed on them. It was the one reproach that was always guaranteed to hit home, and the teacher, whose name and face have long been erased from my memory, knew that she could count on its effect. Feeling shame and guilt that my behavior should have smeared the blameless name of my parents, I would inevitably burst into tears. My sorrow was not so much for what I had done or not done. It was rather because I was incapable of finding a satisfactory reply to silence my tormentor forever and because my parents had been called to account unjustly. Whatever I had done I knew was my own responsibility, not theirs, and I was only too aware that I had fallen as short of their standards as I had of the teacher's.

I feel similar despair when I find that someone's belief or otherwise hinges on the question of suffering in the world. Just as I knew that my parents were wonderful people who should not be judged by my behavior, so I know that the wonders of God should not be judged by the shortcomings of ordinary mortals. But how to convince others of this?

Even greater desperation sets in when the question about suffering comes from a small child in the form: "Why does God allow all this suffering?" Here the problem is not one of God or not God, but of a good God or a mysterious God. And you know that the child is growing up, has begun to question and will no longer accept easy answers from soothing parents. He or she is tearing to be off on his or her own journey of discovery with its share of suffering ahead.

One of the most simple answers must be that God is not a celluloid Superman who holds up crumbling dams, pastes back the earthquake cracks, forces missiles off their path, stops helicopters crashing to the ground and kills the terrible tyrant just in time to save mankind from disaster. Superman is the modern projection of human wishes and needs, of our longing for supernatural happenings. God is not. Superman would certainly have escaped from the cross, saved the two thieves along with him, rustled up the trembling apostles to defeat the Roman legions and converted the world to instant goodness. God did not and left us limited human beings wondering why. One can't help thinking in reply to Feuerbach that if man had invented God, he wouldn't have left himself struggling with so many questions to answer.

Once, when discussing the credibility of belief in God, a friend turned to me and said, "What about turning the question around for a change and asking yourself whether God believes in you?" I was as stunned as if someone had asked me whether my parents really loved me or not. The thought that they might not love me or that God might not believe in me seemed quite absurd. I, of course, felt that it was my natural right to question both my parents and God, disagree with them, provoke them and even leave them. That they might turn the tables on me was something new; that they might cease to love me or not be there when I needed them didn't seem quite right. What had not dawned on me until then was that a two-way relationship was involved between a child and its parents or between God and human beings.

In some respects I had good enough reasons to be startled. A parent's love for a child does not cease because he or she is trying, difficult, argumentative, selfish, independent. It is not the behavior of the child, whether good or bad, which generates the parent's love. It is something quite beyond externals. The child's behavior may give rise to anger, impatience, despair, concern, happiness, pride, but none of these feelings touch the core of love itself: the wonder and terror in face of the responsibility for another human being. Human love is a miracle which bends to no logic, which depends on no return, which is an unsolicited gift from one person to another. The infinity of divine love must be much more than this. But how often we take it all for granted!

How often our belief in God depends on our own notions and inventions. We want God to conform to our own ideas and patterns. We want him there when we need him, but not to interfere when we decide we don't need him. We want things our way, and when we don't get them we become cross, feel neglected and blame God for making a mess of our lives. How often we reproach him for not living up to our human expectations, like the fisherman at the end of the last chapter who couldn't see the miracle happening under his nose. How often we ask for answers in terms of human logic and fail to find the answers.

As you look forward, Gerald, to the crucifixion, to that moment in time when the suffering of God and man became united for all eternity, I am tempted to look back to where you brought us in—to Job.

Perhaps it was because I felt that I knew the story so well that I had never actually read the book of Job. Now I can say that I only wish I had discovered its beauty and its drama sooner. Its poetry must surely rank alongside that of the better known Song of Solomon. But how often is it read? The name "Job" and the expression "Job's comforters" have crept into our everyday language and imagery. But how many of us know that magnificent passage of Job's search for God (Chapter 23)? The whole structure of the book as a work of literature is perfectly balanced and the drama is so compelling that one almost feels one is watching a play—a *King Lear*, a *Hamlet* or even a *Faust*. The leisurely scene describing Job's riches is followed by the dramatic conversation between Satan and God, the rapid destruction of all Job's possessions, his family and his health. We then move through the poetry of his despair and the inconclusive dialogue with his friends, to his challenge to God to judge him openly, God's conversation with Job from the heart of the whirlwind and then the final prose passage describing the restoration of Job's fortune. In the end it is not so much the well-known suffering of Job which dominates the book. It is rather Job's struggle with

God, echoing Christ's own cry of anguish from the cross, which sets this tragic figure apart.

It is easy to become transfixed by the enormity of Job's unmerited suffering, but it is in what lies beyond this that we have to look for the secret of Job's unflinching belief in God. We may still be puzzled by God's reply, but Job in that wonderful last passage has found his answer. If we are overpowered by the question of suffering, if we stop at Job's laments or later at the horror of Christ's death on the cross, we shall never get through to the revelation of God in the whirlwind or the glory of the Easter resurrection.

4

"Creator of Heaven and Earth"

Christian faith holds that "out of nothing" God has created the whole universe and constantly keeps it in existence. Both in their origin and ongoing life, human beings, our planet and the whole cosmos are utterly dependent on God, the first and ultimate cause of everything and the only being that (in the fullest sense of the word) necessarily exists.

Why believe this doctrine of creation? What makes it credible? Does it link up at all with what we know about ourselves and our universe?

One could work away at the traditional arguments about our existence as contingent beings or beings that do not have to exist. To explain our existence we must postulate the necessary being, the first (uncaused) cause who set everything going and every moment keeps everything from lapsing back into nothingness. For many people, however, more light might be shed on the subject by drawing on the physical and biological sciences.

Take, for example, the widely-held scientific view about the origin of the universe, the Big Bang theory, according to which the whole physical universe came into existence in a kind of cosmic explosion about fifteen billion years ago. There was no pre-existent matter that would allow us to speak about the situation "before" the Big Bang nor about this cosmic-sized bang happening "somewhere." Instead, at the Big Bang, space and time themselves came into being with the material universe. As they peer back into the past, scientists stop at that point. For many who draw conclusions from science, however, the Big Bang theory and the evidence supporting it seem to indicate the original moment of creation when the Creator (who exists "outside" the limits of space and time) brought our universe into existence.

Not everyone is willing to draw that conclusion. Some scientists point to the subatomic world where particles apparently come into being out of nowhere and with no clear cause bringing them into existence. They then argue from the microcosm to the macrocosm. If subatomic particles can apparently turn up from nowhere without a prior cause being responsible for these events, perhaps the very universe simply generated itself spontaneously in the Big Bang—without a "prior" (divine) agent bringing this about. Notable scientists hold this view. But I must confess to feeling that they move here in an unjustified way from the microcosm to the macrocosm. It is one thing to note that some particles come into existence without our being able (so far?) to establish the cause. It is quite another thing to suggest that the entire physical universe just brought itself into being out of nothing—without any "prior" cause being involved. With all due deference to great physicists, I fail to see how they justify a self-generating universe and not accept that their Big Bang theory heavily favors the existence of a divine cause of everything.

What of the present physical universe and scientific discoveries about the laws by which it works? There is some apparent anarchy at the subatomic level and enough seeming chaos around to produce theories bearing that name. Nevertheless, the universe is no chaotic mess, but one in which the speed of light remains uniform in all frames of reference and in which particles like protons behave in exactly the same way everywhere. Why is the extremely complex universe so orderly? Why are there laws of nature at all? Add too the fact that minute changes in the laws of physics would have made the emergence of human life and all life impossible. These laws do not seem to be an accidental set that just happened to be that way, but rather finely organized so that eventually human life could come on the scene. Why are there precisely *these* laws of physics, without which we would not have emerged and could not exist? Is this universe just a gigantic accident that happened by chance to be governed by the present laws and so produced human beings in the relatively brief time available after the Big Bang? Or is there a personal designer who purposefully organized the universe and its laws to bring us about?

The fascinating findings and theories of the new physics cannot be simply pressed into service to prove the existence of a divine creator. Here, as always, faith in God remains a free choice and cannot be publicly and scientifically demonstrated. Nevertheless, modern physics serves at the very least to enhance our wonder over the extraordinary history and structure of this universe. From that sense of wonder it is a short step to faith's vision of the creator.

Something like that is true in the field of biology or life-science. Modern research has uncovered the orderly and purposeful complexity of living organisms—with the promise that even more extraordinary things are still to be discovered about the way such organisms function. Take, for example, the human nervous system: twelve billion cells, each one of which has up to sixty thousand points of connection with other cells. This nervous system, which is as complex a physical object as there is in the whole universe, functions in an orderly and efficient way that leaves far behind the most sophisticated products of electronic engineering. Faced with the latest computers and computer-programs, we naturally ask about the designers and the programers. It is hardly surprising that one concludes to a designer when biology over and over again confronts us with the highly unified and purposeful functioning of extraordinarily complex living organisms.

Some evidence from the Religious Experience Research Unit in Oxford and other sources suggests, however, that the move in faith from the world around us to the creator is not normally triggered by the work of modern physics and biology. People spontaneously reach up to God from the simple beauty of nature: an English garden at sunset, the play of light on a clear stream, the silent majesty of a desert, the sights and sounds on the Cornish coast, the intricate glory and variety of flowers. The commonest and simplest things of nature lead people beyond —to acknowledge nature's origin in God. It is not a logical deduction that affirms an uncaused cause of everything, but rather an intuitive sense of the personal presence and power to which nature bears witness.

When the topic of creation comes up, some Christians still attempt to inflict on the unsuspecting public their anti-evolutionary views and fundamentalistic interpretations of the Genesis story. What does the Bible really say here?

The Jewish people originally learned about God not from what they observed in nature but from what they experienced in their own history. An early creed that we find in Deuteronomy 26:5–10 recalls the saving deeds of God in history without adding a word as such about creation:

A wandering Aramean was my father; and he went down into Egypt and sojourned there, few in number; and there he became a nation, great, mighty and populous. And the Egyptians treated us harshly, and afflicted us, and laid upon us hard bondage. Then we cried to the Lord the God of our fathers, and the Lord heard our voice, and saw our affliction, our toil, and our oppression; and the Lord brought us out of Egypt with a mighty hand and an outstretched arm, with great terror, with signs and wonders; and he brought us into this place and gave us this land, a land flowing with milk and honey.

From faith in God whom they knew in their history and with whom they were bound through a special covenant, the Israelites came to recognize also God's hand in the making of the world (for example, Pss 74:13–17; 89:10–13; 119:89–91). The classic passage about creation is, of course, Genesis 1:1–2:4; to that we now turn.

Far from describing here *how* the world began, the Bible has other things to say. God freely and powerfully created all things. Called into being by God's word, the universe is totally good, not a dualistic zone of conflict between good and evil forces. As the crown of creation, human beings were made in the divine image to obey God freely and be responsible stewards of creation. The Genesis story is interested in the end product (the world created by God) rather than the starting point. Eventually the Bible speaks of the starting point: God creating out of nothing (2 Mac 7:28). But apropos of creation, the scriptures are much more concerned to encourage believers to know and praise God through whose free and loving initiative all things came into being (Wis 13:1–9; Pss 8; 19; 24; 33; 104 etc.).

The question of evolution simply does not surface in the Bible. From the point of view of faith, however, the thesis of evolution offers an admirable picture of the divine design that worked itself out in the aftermath of the Big Bang. From the inside—in and through the given laws of nature—God brought about on this planet the emergence of life and ultimately the arrival of human beings. Hence I simply do not understand what so-called "creationists" hope to achieve by reading into the biblical text a non-existent opposition to the theory of evolution. This theory is recent and still deficient in some details. Yet believers can properly find in it a fascinating tribute to the

41

wisdom and power of the creator who works "from the inside" on the divinely created world.

Before finishing this chapter, I should add something about the responsibility for the world which the Genesis story briefly but clearly indicates. For as long as I can remember, some words of my maternal grandfather represented for me such a sense of stewardship—at least toward my nation and continent. As a member of the Australian Federal Convention (1897–99), he introduced into the preamble of our constitution the phrase "humbly relying on the blessing of Almighty God."

On the one hand, these words were intended to express the Jewish-Christian faith and trust in God as creator. On the other hand, they introduced what followed: the political duties, rights and responsibilities accepted by all those who gave and give allegiance to the Australian constitution.

A friend in Nuremberg came at the issue in another way. "Nature is a gift to us. But we rarely see pure nature as it emerged through an evolutionary process from the hands of God. In the whole of Germany we have only about ninety acres in a Bavarian forest where nature is untouched and the trees grow as they like. The rest of our forests are products of culture. The trees march up and down in straight lines—like the Prussian soldiers of Frederick the Great." He paused and went on: "Modern medicine and hygiene have changed us too. Along with our habitat and social structures, we human beings have become at least partly products of our own culture. But it doesn't matter what the precise mix is between nature and culture. My point is *this*. Under God we should act as wise stewards toward ourselves and our environment. The gift of creation brings with it a radical obligation. We can act responsibly or else mess everything up, ourselves included."

Over and beyond the particular issue of creation, my friend's remarks illustrate something that runs through the entire Creed. To *confess* some article of faith (here God as creator) implies a personal *commitment* (in this case toward ourselves and the world around us).

After creation the Apostles' Creed moves us on to Christ and the salvation he brought. The Hebrew scriptures had already linked creation and the history of salvation. As much or more than any section of the Old Testament, the second part of Isaiah (40–66) celebrated *together* the God who had called everything into existence and the Lord of Israel's history:

> Thus says God, the Lord who created the heavens and stretched them out, who spread forth the earth and what comes from it, who gives breath to the people upon it and spirit to those who walk in it: "I am the Lord. I have called you in righteousness. I have taken you by the hand and kept you" (Is 42:5–6).

In various ways the Christian scriptures linked creation and redemption, not least by picturing Christ as the new Adam, "the image of the invisible God, the first-born of all creation" (Col 1:15) who is "the likeness of God" (2 Cor 4:4).

Before moving on to Christ and redemption, I want to add a comparison that can illuminate our relationship with the creator God in whom "we live and move and have our being" (Acts 17:28). Before birth we were all completely dependent on our mother for life, nourishment and growth. In her we lived and moved and had our being. She surrounded us and kept us in existence every moment. Yet it was only after our birth that our eyes were opened to see her. Can we think of our relationship to God as being now somewhat like that? Living, as it were, in the divine womb, we find in the creator our constant habitat and ever-present source of existence. When born into the world to come, our eyes will be opened and we will finally see that mothering God in whom we have always lived and moved and had our being.

43

For several days now your chapter has sent me wandering through the sequences of the Big Bang theory (a name which financiers and stockbrokers have now adopted from scientists), the double helix in DNA and RNA, the nucleus of the living cell and the imponderables of genetic engineering. All are areas of research which are destined to affect our understanding of creation and offer new explanations and interpretations of our life here on earth. These recent discoveries will probably change patterns of twenty-first century thought as much as Darwin's theory of evolution revolutionized nineteenth century thinking.

But my explorations along the fringes of modern science leave me dissatisfied. Perhaps progress and change in these fields during the last two decades have been too rapid for me to keep up with. Or perhaps after fifteen years in Italy the senses have come to play a more important part in my life than the more rational and linear reasoning so characteristic of northern Europe and America. There is a directness of approach in the north which is quite lacking further south. Anyone who has lived in Italy will have discovered that Italians rarely ask those direct questions so common in the Anglo-Saxon world. They feel their way cautiously, without necessarily asking what you do, where you live, or even your name, until you end up good friends without knowing many precise details about the other person. You discover that the facts don't necessarily matter; it is the feeling that counts.

So I turn away from science and look to art in my search for God the creator. In Rome there could be no more appropriate place to start the journey than the Sistine Chapel—an almost compulsory stop for anyone passing through the Eternal City.

Michelangelo's Creation lies along the ceiling of the Chapel, a much more difficult place to work and even to see than the upright wall of the Last Judgment. We know something of the effort the Creation cost the great Florentine painter who worked in back-breaking conditions and often without much light. He had none of the modern equipment available to the team of restorers now completing their work on his masterpiece. Something of the artist's feeling—the labor, anxiety and worry—are caught in the face of God as he stretches out to give life to the limp and almost listless figure of Adam.

To look at Michelangelo's God is to be reminded that creation, however large or small, is not something that just happens. It requires an act of will, an act of commitment, a conscious act of dedication, perhaps suffering, certainly hard work and hopefully love. For all this it may remain totally unappreciated. Compared with the face of God as he looks to Adam, there is not much feeling in Adam's expression as he turns to face his maker.

The essence of creation is not something that can be restrained within the bounds of scientific theory, however much we may long for an easy, provable formula. Each act of creation, whether a new human being, work of art or scientific theory, is unique. A part is explainable in scientific, biological or technical terms but a part is not. A great painting is no more reducible to the artist and his materials than a new-born child is just the sum of its parents. The two are bound but they are separate; the hands of God and Adam on the ceiling of the Sistine Chapel reach for each other but they do not touch.

The act of creation is a separation of the created from the creator as form is molded from formlessness. For nine months a mother and her child are entirely dependent on each other as blood and liquid flow between them. But in order for both to live they must, quite literally, be cut apart. If they are not, the one or the other will die. For two beings birth is only the beginning of a long and sometimes difficult separation from each other: from breast feeding through weaning, crawling, walking, education and beyond.

In nature the process is similar. The living cell divides, separates and specializes to perform its own function. In the world of art the moment also arrives when the completed work has to stand apart from its creator. How many novelists, poets, painters, composers have agonized over their work to be amazed or even shocked by the reaction of the public to the finished masterpiece! How many different readings can there be of a poem, a play, a symphony, an opera, which move beyond what the artist ever imagined!

In the creation story in the first chapter of Genesis—a story which surprisingly follows a precise evolutionary pattern as God first moves across the waters, indispensable to any form of life, then creates light out of darkness, dry land, vegetation, lower forms of life in the water, land animals and then last of all man—it is as man is separated from God and then woman from man that human beings begin to live out their existence as individuals. It is finally in an act contrary to God's will that the full implications of God's creation—the separation of God and man and man's unique responsibility for his own actions—become clear.

Just as in human birth and then family life it is the child who strikes out on his own, so in the relationship of God with man it is man who makes the first move away. But just as the growing physical and psychological independence of the child from the parents in no way diminishes the anxiety of the parents for their creation, so God's constant concern for his people is evident throughout the Bible. Time and again in the history of the Jewish people God's saving presence is apparent. It is as though the responsibilities inherent in creation, a unique event in itself, were constantly renewed and reaffirmed in manifestations of love for the created. Creation is a statement of belief and an act of love for which the creator is constantly responsible to a greater (divine) or lesser (human) extent regardless of the feelings or behavior of the created.

Left to ourselves we tend to make a mess of things. The first story in the Bible after Adam and Eve are ban-

46

ished from the garden of Eden is the one of Cain and Abel —a story of human jealousy ending in murder. For a modern illustration we need only read William Golding's *Lord of the Flies* or walk into a classroom when the teacher is absent to understand what happens when the guiding hand is removed.

You mention how the beauty of nature brings many to an awareness of God's creation. Perhaps it was your reference to an English garden or those wonderful passages in the writings of St. Teresa of Avila which encouraged me to think of the role of a gardener in the work of creation. It is the gardener, even more than the beholder of the garden's beauty, who really knows both the marvels and the dangers of nature. It is he who molds beauty out of a wilderness. He knows the needs of each flower and plant: the right quantities of light and shade, sand or peat, exposure or protection; the advantages of the north- or south-facing wall. He watches the growth of each shoot and seedling and is glad when a withered plant gives signs of life. It is the gardener who weeds, digs and prunes, who despairs when the plants are eaten by insects, seared by the winds, destroyed by marauding animals, drowned by excessive rain or burnt by an unexpected drought.

The labor in a garden is constant, and a gardener knows, as no observer knows, that if he rests, the wilderness will return and the beauty of his creation will be gone. Creation for the gardener is not just the planting in spring —that initial Big Bang of science. It carries through the abundance of the summer growth, the splendor of the autumn brilliance, the patient vigil in the dead of winter, to return full cycle to another spring.

5

"Jesus Christ,
His Only Son, Our Lord"

When I returned to Italy last August, a profes-
sional writer took me out for an evening meal
in a Roman trattoria. In his youth a conscious decision had
taken him away from the Catholic faith. More than twenty
years later a religious experience in New York put him
back on the road to a deep life of belief.

Outside the trattoria the humid evening turned to
rain as the writer probed himself and me with questions
about the God in whom we believe. He had been reading
some contemporary scientists for whom the intricate balance of the universe points to a mysterious power behind
it all. "There's a link between these scientists and some
mystical writers," he exclaimed. "But they leave us with a
God who is wonderful and even beautiful, but so rarefied
and remote."

The birth of Christ bridged the gap between the apparently remote God and ourselves. But even before that
happened, God was (and is) no lonely deity but always
tripersonal: Father, Son and Holy Spirit. That evening in
Rome I should have brought up the topic of the Trinity.

To express their belief that God is not only one being
but also three persons in relation, Christians have pressed
into service various schemes of thought. The Father loves
the Son, and the Spirit is the mutual love between Father

and Son. Our God is lover, beloved and personified love, the ultimate "I, thou and we" in the universe.

Of course, it took the life, death and resurrection of Jesus to let us into the secret about God being not only one but also tripersonal. Christians make the sign of the cross "in the name of the Father, and of the Son and of the Holy Spirit." In doing that they associate their faith in the tripersonal God above all with the dying and rising of Jesus. We will come back to that later. For the moment let us reflect on what the Apostles' Creed initially encourages us to believe about God's "only Son" even before he was "born of the Virgin Mary."

Within the eternal life of God, the Son is the perfect image of the Father, even to the point of completely sharing one and the same nature as the Father. From the fourth century Christians professed this truth by calling the Son "of one being" with the Father. John's gospel is getting at the same point when Jesus declares, "He who has seen me has seen the Father" (Jn 14:9).

During his brief ministry Jesus surprised and shocked people by implying that he enjoyed a unique relationship of equality with the God whom he addressed with great familiarity as "Abba" or "Father dear." Eventually his habit of giving the impression of being on a par with God led the religious authorities in Jerusalem to accuse him of blasphemy.

The Creed behind this book simply speaks of Jesus as God's "only Son." *By itself* this phrase could take on various meanings. It could, for example, be misunderstood to envisage the Son being brought into existence subsequently and so not being on an absolute par with the Father. To obviate such misunderstandings early Christian statements insisted that "there never was a time when he was not" (= the Son was/is always there with the Father). He was "begotten but not made" by the Father (= the Son came from but was not created by the Father).

In an age that has rightly become more sensitive

about sexist language it is good to note the feminine terminology that has also been applied to the relationship between the first and second divine persons. John's gospel speaks of "the only Son who is in the bosom of the Father" (Jn 1:18). Some centuries later the Eleventh Council of Toledo (in Spain) left us a long creed which presented the Son as being generated "from the womb of the Father."

Thus far I have concentrated on the phrase about Jesus being the "Son" of God. But the whole article of the Creed we are considering in this chapter says more about Jesus of Nazareth by applying three titles to him. He is the Christ or promised deliverer of his people. He is "Son of God" in an utterly unique and exclusive way. (Other human beings can only be brought into God's family as adopted sons and daughters.) Third, Jesus is "our Lord" whose divine identity and status merits our worship.

Clearly the first claim about Jesus poses fewer problems. People who suffer from death, meaninglessness and hatred (in their different forms) can hope that God will appoint and send them a deliverer or "Christ." But that the deliverer will prove to be the only Son of God and divine Lord is obviously a difficult and mysterious claim.

Historically the Jewish people had various expectations about one or more deliverers coming from God. Often the "messiah" or "Christ" was understood to be a king from David's line who would save the suffering people. Alongside hopes about a kingly messiah, there were other messianic expectations. A classic example is that of an agent of salvation who, while not being a king, would nevertheless be authorized by God to deliver those who suffered. In the second part of Isaiah we read: "The Spirit of the Lord God is upon me, because the Lord has anointed me to bring good tidings to the afflicted; he has sent me to bind up the brokenhearted, to proclaim liberty to the captives and the opening of the prison to those who are bound" (Is 61:1). We find these and other messianic hopes recorded in the Old Testament. The new and surprising thing is not so much that these hopes were fulfilled but that the deliverer turned out to be the Son of God in person.

In dialogue with their Jewish friends Christians need to account for their belief that Jesus of Nazareth is "the Christ" or messianic deliverer appointed by God. Did the history and hopes of Israel find their point and purpose in Jesus and history? After reading the Jewish scriptures, do we find in the gospels the sense of an ending?

At the same time we should note how the Apostles' Creed presents Jesus not only as the Christ but even as the Son of God who should be worshiped and followed as divine Lord. What justifies giving Jesus those two further titles? At the origins of Christianity believers came to acknowledge him in those terms, above all because their experience of his power and presence as risen from the dead could not honestly be satisfied with anything less. Undoubtedly other factors (like the memory of what Jesus had said and done during his earthly ministry) also encouraged the early Christians to recognize Jesus as Son of God and Lord. Nevertheless, the major catalyst for that faith came from their experiencing his saving power and presence after his resurrection from the dead.

That leaves us today with the questions: Do we find life, meaning and love coming to us through the risen Jesus? Do we experience him delivering us from evil in a way that justifies our acknowledging him as the Son of God and divine Lord?

Any answers to these questions are bound up with our response to what follows in the Creed. After all, "I believe in Jesus Christ, his only Son, our Lord" is just the first of a whole series of propositions about the second person of the Trinity. These propositions all concern either what Jesus has done, from his conception to his being "seated at the right hand of the Father," or will do when he comes again "to judge the living and the dead." What we make of all those subsequent affirmations about his activity will decide whether we give our allegiance to Jesus of Nazareth as messianic deliverer, the only Son of God and our divine Lord.

In a sense the basic commitment proposed by the article we are considering is focused by the very name, "Jesus," which means "God is salvation." The first Christians experienced salvation coming through Jesus to the point that they felt constrained to call him the only Son of God and divine Lord. In the New Testament the term "savior" is only used of God (eight times) and of Jesus (sixteen times). No one else is called "savior" by the Christian scriptures. Today the question for us is likewise built into Jesus' name. Do we experience deliverance from sin and evil and the gift of divine blessings being mediated to us through Jesus to the extent that we must acknowledge him as the savior and Lord who is truly divine?

Our basic enemies are as old as the human race itself: death in all its forms (including the self-destructiveness of sin), meaninglessness, and isolation or even hatred. The staggeringly new claim of Christianity is that, through the resurrection of a crucified first century Galilean, life, meaning and love (both here and hereafter) are offered to the whole human race.

Those who already accept and experience the truth of this claim recognize Jesus as the only Son of God and our divine Lord. Those for whom Jesus and deliverance through him are still alien will find it hard to gauge the Christian claim. Until they meet believers whose new existence strikingly testifies to the truth of their faith, "outsiders" will probably lack the grace to visualize what accepting Jesus as deliverer, Son of God and divine Lord could be like. The following chapters may, however, throw some more light on the truth about Jesus' activity and identity.

In any case what now follows about the birth, life, death and resurrection of Jesus will be concerned, at least in part, with human history. It will, I hope, mitigate the feeling shared by my host in the Roman trattoria and many others that God is wonderful but remote. The eternal Son of God became flesh in Mary's womb to be eventually known for what he was and is—Emmanuel or God with us (Mt 1:23).

Probably at no other time in history would the words "rarefied and remote" have been used as a criticism of God. Certainly in the nineteenth century and before that, remoteness was a normal condition of everyday life. Parents were remote from their children, kings and queens from their subjects, politicians from their electorate and employers from their employees.

In the second half of the twentieth century it is wrong to be remote, whatever other wonderful qualities may be hidden under a seemingly distant façade. Popes are no longer carried through crowds: they mingle with believers whenever possible. The few remaining western monarchs seem fairly ordinary human beings. Fathers, once awesome, seldom-seen figures, now change nappies, cook meals and take their children to school.

That we should seek a closer God is therefore hardly surprising. Words such as powerful, mighty, supreme judge and even king are used less and less to describe God. Expressions such as friend, counselor, guide and helper come more easily.

In line with our efforts to find a less remote God, films on the life of Jesus appear with amazing frequency. Now that the gospel stories are no longer confined to the pages of the Bible, accessible only to the literate and the interested, more people than ever before are familiar with certain aspects of the birth, life, death and resurrection of Jesus. While church attendance continues to fall, controversy over the latest film-interpretation of the life of

Christ hits the front pages of the newspapers, drawing an ever wider audience into the discussion. We search for the real image of Christ in the Shroud of Turin, and hang on to bits and pieces of history in order to bring the human Jesus closer.

The advantages of this are clear. Gaps have been bridged which would have seemed inconceivable only a few decades ago. But are there dangers too?

We live in a camera-happy age in which we can record almost any moment from before birth to death. Photos, however, tell a selective tale. For millions the war in Vietnam will always be symbolized by the screaming, naked girl burning with napalm. But how many of those who know her face also know her name or what has happened to her since? John Kennedy's children will always be remembered as they were on the day of his burial, not as they are now. The first pictures of the moon will be remembered for a clumsy-looking Neil Armstrong, not for the landscape of earth's mysterious satellite.

At the more personal level, if you put up a photo of an absent or dead friend or relation, after a while the face seems to dominate and the personality to fade in your memory. You tend to remember just the face, captured in a second of time. Without the photo, probably not a very good likeness anyway, you may not remember the face as clearly as before, but perhaps you will recall the real person better.

Has the filmed Jesus, our favorite picture of him or the image on the Shroud of Turin become like the face in the photo? Our son, then seven years old, hit on the problem one day when he said he knew twenty-six Jesuses. Taken by surprise I asked him why twenty-six, to which he replied that there was the one at school, the one in the church, the one above his bed, the one in the cinema, the one in the musical, the one on television, the one in his head and so on. It would be nice, he said, to know which was the real one. For him Jesus is certainly no remote being, but to find the real one among all the imagery of the twentieth century is no easy task.

In this image-conscious era it is difficult to go back to those first, concise principles in the Creed. They seem so stark, bleak, reductive and difficult to comprehend. As I read your chapter I began to wonder where my familiar, flesh-and-blood and ever-loving Jesus had gone. The film images, the Shroud, my favorite paintings, my speculative wanderings through the gospels in search of the earthly Jesus all came to an abrupt end. There I was at the end of the chapter with all the trappings gone, face to face with the bare and remote reality: Jesus Christ, Son and Lord. In a way it was like returning to the pure lines of northern gothic after a self-indulgent surfeit of glorious, southern baroque.

In all their simplicity these few words contain the essence of Christianity, the point where Christians are forced to leave their Jewish heritage behind. It is just possible that the old covenant could have embraced Jesus the savior as the longed-for and long-heralded messiah. But there was no room for the Son of God. God for the Jews, then and now, was and is without form or physical substance. God could not therefore become man without revolutionizing the whole Jewish faith. That God should have a Son was folly enough; that the Son should take human form was madness; that he should be both man and God was blasphemy.

It is perhaps not surprising therefore that Jesus drew his early followers, up until the conversion of Paul, not from within the confines of the religious hierarchy but from the fringes of the Jewish people, from those who were not so steeped in the old covenant that they were not open to the new. The conversion of Paul, a Pharisee and a Roman citizen, marked a momentous milestone in the spread of Christianity—the first opening of the establishment doors. But Paul became a Christian only after the true identity of Jesus was revealed in the resurrection.

Paul never followed the man in the same sense that Peter and the other apostles had done, coming closer to God in the footsteps of the living Jesus.

As we come to accept Jesus as the Son of God it becomes essential to worship him as Lord, just as if we reject Jesus as the Son of God it is absurd to worship him as Lord. The two are inseparably linked and the latter depends on the former. How we come to believe in Jesus Christ as the Son of God is revealed, as you have pointed out, by what follows in the rest of the Creed.

However, before we move on to explain why we believe as we do, there are still two words, seemingly insignificant in their ordinariness, which capture not only the mystery but also the immediacy of Christianity and inspire a sense of marvel at the genius of the Creed's writers. In the two possessive pronouns *his* and *our*—*his* only Son, *our* Lord—we have the root of the Christian faith.

Jesus is both God's and ours. Had he been exclusively the Son of God, then he would not have been ours in the same way. Had he been only ours, then he would not have been divine. Instead, in Jesus Christ, his only Son, our Lord, the separation of man from God is finally brought to an end. The hands of God and Adam meet in the Bethlehem stable.

6

"He Was Conceived by the Power of the Holy Spirit"

Without troubling to hear more about Jesus, some may damn the Christian story for turning preposterous right at the outset. What value could anyone find in the claim made by Matthew, Luke and the Creed that Jesus was conceived by a woman not through sexual intercourse with a human father but through a mysterious intervention of the Holy Spirit? Surely one should admit that this did not really happen and that Christians simply adapted some pagan story about a male deity impregnating a woman and so producing an extraordinary child? Isn't talk about being conceived through the Holy Spirit non-factual and merely a roundabout way of claiming that Jesus, while beginning his human history in a perfectly normal way, was personally divine, the only Son of God come among us?

One of these questions can be dealt with at once. Non-Christian stories about male gods impregnating human women do not offer anything like close parallels to what we read in the gospels of Matthew and Luke. Those pagan stories involve sexual activity, something that is noticeably lacking in what Matthew and Luke say about Jesus being conceived by the power of the Holy Spirit. There is no hard evidence for the thesis that in their account of Jesus' origins Christians took over a pagan story about a male deity impregnating a woman.

What of the view that "conceived by the power of the Holy Spirit" is not telling us about anything that happened but should be decoded as simply a way of expressing faith in Jesus as divine? Those who take this view often seem to presuppose a false alternative: conception through the Holy Spirit is *either* factual *or* a way of acknowledging Jesus as being divine. But why not both? Something can truly happen and at the same time be also a way of speaking of God and God's intentions. Take Jesus' crucifixion. It is an historical fact which expresses many things, not least God's utterly generous love toward us.

Of course, one can object that a crucifixion is nothing extraordinary. The Romans, the Carthaginians and others crucified thousands of unfortunate victims. A conception through the power of the Holy Spirit is, on any showing, a miraculous intervention by God. Then the question becomes: Does God ever intervene in such ways, to alter the normal functioning of natural causes? Did God once act in a special way to bring about the conception of a male child (Jesus) without the male parent (Joseph) being involved? For all the differences between the opening chapters of their gospels, Matthew and Luke are at one in testifying that Jesus was not conceived through ordinary sexual intercourse but through a special act of God. Once we accept that there is a God who has created the whole universe and constantly keeps it in existence, it does not seem odd to believe that for wise and loving reasons, the creator may at times intervene in miraculous ways in the normal working of nature. The case in point is Jesus' miraculous conception.

Thus far I have tried to sketch a case for the *fact* of Jesus' virginal conception. As all-powerful creator of the universe, God *could* wisely and lovingly intervene to do something like that. Matthew, Luke and subsequent Christians testify that this *has happened.* The two gospel writers refer to the conception of Jesus from different standpoints—Matthew from that of Joseph, Luke from

58

that of Mary. But both authors concur that this conception did not come about through normal sexual intercourse. Without indulging flights of biological fantasy, they attribute Jesus' conception to a special, miraculous intervention of the Holy Spirit.

I suspect that for a number of people the problem is not so much in admitting the core claim being made by Matthew, Luke and the Christian tradition about the origins of Jesus' human life but rather in finding any deep religious significance in it. The virginal conception of Jesus will remain low on the credibility scale unless they see some real value in this article of faith. What religious meaning can and does this event convey to us?

Stripped to its simplest terms, the virginal conception of Jesus expresses his personal identity. The fact that he had no human father points to his eternal life and status at the divine level—as the only Son of God. The history of Christianity bears witness to this key to interpretation. Believers have always understood the virginal conception of Jesus as one of the major events that reflect and express his divinity. We can sum up the significance of the event this way: conceived by the Holy Spirit Jesus is truly divine; born of a woman (Mary) he was and is truly human.

Some people fear that while signifying very well the divinity of Jesus, his virginal conception makes his real humanity rather doubtful from the outset. If his human story began through a miraculous intervention of the Holy Spirit, that event sets him apart from the rest of human beings. Their life begins with an act of sexual intercourse that leads to their conception. Granted that a virginal conception made Jesus' human origin substantially (although not completely) different from ours, how can one continue to maintain that he was and is fully human?

Before responding, let me note how other items in the story of Jesus also give rise to the same question. For instance, he lived a life free from sin, worked miracles for the sick and others, and rose from the dead to become the

59

effective savior of the whole world. Being sinless, possessing miraculous powers and becoming savior of the world lift Jesus above and beyond what we know to be a "normal" human existence. Nevertheless, both here and in the case of his being virginally conceived the answer is the same. He did not have to be *merely* human in order to be *fully* human. Or to phrase matters slightly differently, he did not have to correspond to us "normal" human beings in all ways, in order to be fully human. The history of very many men and women takes them through marriage, the raising of children, retirement and old age—experiences which Jesus did not share. He grew up physically and mentally, thought, took decisions, felt deep emotions, wept, ate, drank, entered into personal relationships, talked, suffered and eventually died. These and further facts about him justify us in recognizing him as fully human, even if his conception through the Holy Spirit and what it pointed to (his personal identity as Son of God) show that he was not and is not merely human.

We can also make sense of Jesus' virginal conception by seeing its link to what would come at the end. In his beginning was his end. By themselves his miraculous conception and life in his mother's womb come across as the mystery of an unfinished plot. The story would conclude with his death, burial and resurrection from the tomb, that vessel which received his torn body and like a womb held it for three days. The beginning and the end of Jesus' earthly history correspond. Through a special divine intervention, that history began in Mary's womb. It closed with his resurrection from the vessel of the tomb, the final mystery that brought Jesus' followers to recognize him as being truly the Son of God and divine Lord. To be sure, we can say that only one person (Mary) witnessed at first-hand the virginal conception, whereas those who saw the risen Christ made up a group of several hundred witnesses. Nevertheless, the virginal conception at the beginning and the resurrection at the end are of a piece in pointing to Jesus' divine identity as the Son of God.

Matthew associates the beginning and the end by calling Jesus "Emmanuel," which means God with us (Mt 1:23). Right from his conception and birth, Jesus actualized and expressed God's presence to the people. Then at the end of the gospel the risen Christ met his disciples as the one to whom "all authority in heaven and on earth has been given" and who promises: "I am with you always, to the close of the age" (Mt 28:18–20). What Jesus became through his resurrection he had already been from his miraculous conception: the fulfilled expression of God's fatherly and motherly presence with the people.

Up to this point I have been exploring what Jesus' virginal conception can mean in his relationship to God the Father. The event also yields meaning about his relationship to the Holy Spirit.

Christians experienced the aftermath of Jesus' resurrection. They recognized that the Spirit sent to them (*by* the risen Christ or *in his name*) had been actively present in the whole of his life—not only at the start of his ministry but even right back to his conception. In other words, the risen Jesus actively blessed his followers with the Spirit. But in his entire earthly existence he himself had been blessed by the Spirit—right from his conception when he began his earthly existence through the Spirit's creative power.

Thus the event of the virginal conception helps to reveal and clarify the ultimate truth. From its beginning to its end the story of Jesus speaks to us of a God who is tripersonal. His total history discloses the God who is Father, Son and Holy Spirit.

Finally, there is the overarching divine plan to transform human beings and their world through the Holy

Spirit. There the resurrection helps to illuminate the meaning of the virginal conception in that all-embracing history.

St. Paul stretches language to the limit when he speaks of resurrection bringing about the life of the "spiritual body" (1 Cor 15:44). At first glance, the term can seem a contradiction in terms, like a "square circle." If it is a body, it cannot be spiritual. If it is spiritual, it cannot be a body. What the apostle has in mind, however, is a risen bodily existence that will be brought about by the Holy Spirit. In that state we will be spiritualized and live under the power of the Holy Spirit without ceasing to be material and bodily. From the original creation right through to the new creation of resurrection and the final consummation of the world, God's Spirit is at work transforming and spiritualizing human beings, their history and their universe. In that all-embracing history which the Spirit is guiding and shaping, the virginal conception of Jesus is one of the major landmarks along the way.

I remember when I was about eleven my father showed me a scaled plan for his new garden. He explained where the roses would go, where he had planned a bank of azaleas, the clump of camellia trees, the lawns and the borders. All the colors blended in his scheme. The height of the flowers, bushes and trees had been taken into account, the vistas mapped out and the hedges planned against the prevailing winds. It all looked perfect and precisely logical but I couldn't get the feel of the garden from the graph paper. My father knew what he was doing, but I wasn't able to understand the beauty of his project until I saw the garden grow and come alive.

I felt something of this again as I read your chapter. While I loved its harmony and symmetry I wanted to feel the pain, the anxiety, the happiness and the emotion of Mary and Joseph at the moment of the annunciation in order to understand their faith and commitment to God. It is at this moment of conception that both literally and metaphorically God's design for human beings comes alive.

Here the Word becomes flesh and the Spirit forms a body, a body destined to transform our own physical and spiritual existence. What happens to that body (it will be born, grow, die and rise again) is not mere historical curiosity; it is of vital importance to the followers of Christ.

The words "conceived by the power of the Holy Spirit" are giving us here, early in the Creed, the third element of the Trinity. After God the Father and God the Son we now have God the Holy Spirit. And at this moment before the birth of Christ, just as again after his resurrection, we have the Holy Spirit revealing the divine power through the actions of human beings. On both these occasions we have evidence of happenings which defy normal explanations. But we also have evidence of the capabilities of ordinary mortals when graced by the power of the Holy Spirit. Jesus was conceived and carried in a human womb. While the virginal conception tells us of the Trinity, it also tells us of the relationship between God and man.

Time and again in the history of the Jewish people—whether during the exodus from Egypt, the giving of the law, the formation of the kingdom, the exile and return—God chooses ordinary human beings to reveal the divine plan. The great moments in the Old Testament are based on divinely inspired human actions revealing the divine design. Almost without exception the people chosen by God seem ordinary human beings, often ostensibly inadequate to the task they are called to perform. Somehow, miraculously, they rise to their calling, some reluctantly, some fearfully, some doubting their own capacity, some after endless attempts to escape from their task.

In the New Testament God continues to reveal himself in a similar way. It is a very wonderful and humbling sign of God's faith in creation and ordinary human beings that he should have entrusted his Son to a human family for his earthly life. Here God and man come together not only in the person of Jesus but in their mutual trust one for the other. In no other single event has the two-way relationship between God and man been so vividly apparent.

When I reflect on the task given to Joseph and Mary, I gasp at the undertaking they each accepted at the moment of the annunciation. Any woman who has conceived, even under the most ideal circumstances, will know those mixed feelings of joy, excitement, amazement, even disbelief in the early months, the anxiety and the fear at the thought of that new being forming inside her. No mother can help but wonder about her own future and the future of this mysterious, strange new being, desired or undesired as it may be, whom she knows but doesn't know, a part of herself, but not herself, dependent but destined to be independent, a being who will bring pain, responsibility, love, joy and tenderness. Even to understand all this is to understand only a fraction of what Mary must have felt at the annunciation.

There was nothing ideal about her situation at that moment. She was not married, and for a Jewish girl to find herself in a similar situation could have been nothing short of a nightmare. Under normal circumstances it would have been considered a disgrace to her own family, an insult to her future husband's family, and if the future husband were not the father, the offense was punishable by stoning to death.

If we believe as we do that Mary and Joseph, like Adam and Eve before them, were free to accept or reject God's word, then in a very real way the future safety of Mary and her child depended on the decision of Joseph. In the gospel of St. Matthew, Joseph is a shadowy figure. Even in Luke, which contains the longer birth narrative, Joseph is given less space than Elizabeth and Zechariah. In the need to explain the divine origin of Jesus, Joseph has become a figure of secondary importance. But without him Mary would have been at best a permanent outcast

64

from her own community. Given the rules and conventions of the Jewish society of the time, Joseph's acceptance of his divine mission is no less breathtaking than Mary's.

His faith in God, together with his trust in and love for Mary, required a special strength. Not only was he to marry a girl who had already conceived, but he was to marry a girl who had conceived a child not his. While Mary would have had the absolute certainty of the divine origin of her child, Joseph could never have had this certainty in the same way and must have lived his faith in great part through his love for Mary.

Behind the conception of Jesus by the Holy Spirit are two human beings working together in their love for each other to protect the Son of God. It is as though Mary and Joseph, the supreme examples of all that is best in humans —the love, the generosity, the selflessness, the trust in one another—healed the rift between God and man caused by Adam and Eve, the symbols of all that is worst in man: the self-seeking, the deceit, the guile and the betrayal of each other. As Mary and Joseph accept their mission, God's faith in man becomes incarnate.

7

"Born of the Virgin Mary"

Three words—presence, particularity and prayer —gather together much of what I want to say about the birth of Jesus. Let us look first at presence.

Some years ago a friend of mine was complaining about what he took to be the decline and fall of Roman Catholicism in France. His voice faltered as he summed things up: "The French went in for Catholic Action. Then they pushed the line of *témoignage* or witness. Now they are satisfied with mere presence."

At the time I wondered whether my friend was right in being disenchanted with the move from action to witness, and from witness to presence. I put it to myself this way: "When I come to die, no one will be able to do anything for me, and I won't want anyone preaching at me. But I will certainly be reassured by the presence of a close relative or some other person I love dearly."

Nowadays I wonder whether, inadvertently, my friend had stumbled on a good way of expressing the move from creation, through the history of Israel, and down to the birth of Jesus himself. God acted in creation. Moses and the prophets were called to give witness to the people. But Jesus Christ was God's personal presence among us.

In his infancy narrative Matthew calls Jesus "Emmanuel, which means God with us" (Mt 1:25). The prologue of John's gospel climaxes with the announcement: "The

Word became flesh and dwelt among us" (Jn 1:14). This presence came about through the free love of God: "In this was the love of God made manifest among us, that God sent his only Son into the world that we might live through him" (1 Jn 4:9).

Thinking of the Christmas message in terms of a new divine presence carries several advantages. First, we are moving in the area of something we look for every day of our lives—the personal presence of those whom we care for and who care about us. We cannot endure to live friendship and love at a distance. Photographs, memories, letters and even phone calls are not enough. We want to enjoy the personal presence of those who fill our minds and let us live in their hearts. We live in God's heart, and Christmas visibly brought among us the Son of God who cares infinitely for each of us. He did not want to live that love at a distance. He gave us and gives us his personal presence, that most precious gift of those who care for us.

Second, the theme of divine presence has at least a small advantage over some of the other language we use and hear in our worship at Christmas. The reading for the mass at dawn, for example, recalls the birth of Jesus as the time "when the goodness and loving kindness of God our savior appeared" (Tit 3:4). Beyond doubt, this language of "appearance" indicates the divine good will toward human beings. All the same, there is a direct sense of personal relationship communicated by the name "Emmanuel." God is no longer merely "for us" but now "with us." The Word has come to dwell "among us." This presence has initiated a new relationship between the human race and our God. As never before, God is with us and personally related to us.

Third, a personal presence, whether human or divine, always has something mysterious about it. We appreciate the difference between the mere physical nearness of other people on a crowded bus and the supportive presence of a friend at the time of crisis. We are dealing here with something that is utterly real and yet quite difficult to understand and interpret. "Presence" and various kinds of presence can seem a straightforward matter, but on analysis they remain mysteriously elusive. This may partly account for the fact that over the centuries western philosophy has failed to reflect very much on this notion. Apart from Gabriel Marcel (1889–1973) and a few others, philosophers have largely left alone the idea and reality of presence and personal presence.

To speak of the Son of God coming "among us" to live "with us" sounds like simple talk. But we have little help here from the philosophers, and in any case this belief points to a unique mystery, the qualitatively new, personal presence of God in our world.

Fourth, as Vatican II's Constitution on the Sacred Liturgy noted, Christ's personal presence takes different forms (n. 7). This 1963 document naturally addressed itself to the variety of ways Christ becomes present in worship and left it at that. But the link between liturgy and life suggests looking also to the many other forms of Christ's presence around us. In a special way the poor and oppressed bring us his presence. The child in the manger shows us his face in a thousand needy victims of our world. The Christmas message means not only Jesus himself in the arms of Mary but also his presence in the arms of those who carry our suffering brothers and sisters.

I do not know whether my friend feels happier now about the state of French Catholicism. But I remain grateful for the language he offered me. In our human history we find God in action. We hear the prophetic witness given us through the inspired scriptures and inspired speakers. But at Christmas we can rejoice in a uniquely rich and mysterious gift, the new personal presence of "God with us."

Christmas shows us that we contact God not only through what we see and hear but also through what we touch. We can see God acting in history. We can open our ears to hear the divine message to us. But we can also reach out and touch the Son of God, now mysteriously but truly present among us in a rich range of new ways.

My second word about the birth of Jesus is "particularity," a term that assumes a special importance in this context. Let me explain.

From time to time human beings take refuge in a vague religiosity. They accept the existence of God but refuse to believe that at certain fixed points in history God has intervened in a unique way. They pick and choose from various religious traditions, denounce as narrow-minded bigotry any absolute claims and come to believe in their own amalgam of beliefs and fantasies.

The message of Christmas is anything but vague religiosity. It announces that *this* particular baby and *only* this baby has shown us the human face of God. The new-born Jesus looked much like any other Jewish baby of the time. The Christian faith does not argue that this new-born child was larger, more beautiful or stronger than other babies in the neighborhood. It claims something infinitely more important: this baby is God's only Son come among us. Once and for all at a particular point in the story of the only people God ever chose in a special way, during the reign of a specific Roman emperor (Augustus), a child was born who was personally divine and who through his life, death and resurrection would deliver the whole human race from the power of evil.

Reading the opening chapters of the gospels of Matthew and Luke, we can be delighted by the details about the star rising in the east, the baby lying in a manger, and the host of angels appearing to shepherds in the fields. Or else we can be distracted by questions of historical sources and details. Where did Matthew and Luke get the material they used in telling the story of Jesus' birth? Was Luke right about a Roman census that brought Mary to Bethlehem for the birth of her child? Did the appearance of a new comet send the magi on their way to find the child "born to be king of the Jews" (Mt 2:2)? But the heart of the matter for both Matthew and Luke is their witness to the identity and role of this child. He is "Emmanuel, which means God with us" (Mt 1:23), the "savior" (Lk 2:11) born of a Jewish mother at the absolute high-point in the story of God's chosen people.

Through the long journey of the human race, men, women and sometimes whole nations have yearned for God to send someone to guide and deliver them. From time immemorial the search for a deliverer has gone on. What is specifically new in the Christmas story is the good news that on a certain holy night our search ended forever. The deliverer came, a baby who was and is God's only Son. No greater or even comparable savior could ever again be sent us by God.

My third word, "prayer," touches the issue of faith. Why believe that the baby in Mary's arms is the one and only Son of God? How can I justify this faith? A long answer could come through looking at his pre-history in the story of the Jewish people, at the history of his life, death and resurrection, and at his "post-history" in the story of the church—the Jesus-community led by his Spirit and moving toward the end of time when God will make all things new. A short answer can be found in prayer.

In his two volumes, the gospel and the book of Acts, Luke tells the story of Jesus and of the early years of a church that was to witness for Jesus "to the ends of the earth" (Acts 1:8). The two chapters that form the overture to Luke's work gather together some of the greatest Christian prayers: the Magnificat (Lk 1:46–55), the Benedictus (Lk 1:68–79), the angels' song (Lk 2:14), and Simeon's Nunc Dimittis (Lk 2:29–32). No other section in the entire New Testament contains anything like the rich chorus of prayer with which Luke introduces his account of Jesus and the church.

In effect, Luke says to his readers: "If you join Mary, Zechariah, the angels and old Simeon in praising God, you

70

will get the point of my story. I want you to join in the cries of 'My soul glorifies the Lord,' 'Blessed be the Lord, the God of Israel,' and 'Glory to God in the highest.' If you do that, you will be ready to believe in Jesus, the Son of God who brings light and salvation to all peoples" (Lk 2:30–32).

My three words—presence, particularity and prayer —can indicate ways of thinking about Jesus' birth. But it is prayer that is the most valuable pointer. Those who treasure up and in their hearts prayerfully ponder the Christmas story (Lk 2:19, 51) can recognize in faith the real truth about the baby wrapped in swaddling clothes and laid in a manger.

O ccasionally on the birthday of one or other of our children, a relation or a friend, usually a mother herself, will include me in the happy birthday greetings. I find the touch endearing, all the more so because it is not strictly necessary. The birthday, after all, celebrates the advent of the child rather than the role of the mother.

In your chapter above, Gerald, you have in fact reflected on the importance of the central event, the arrival of the baby Jesus, without mentioning the role of Mary. Perhaps it is because I am a mother that my thoughts naturally turn to what Mary must have felt at the birth of Jesus. But it seems more than just idle sentiment to reflect on the importance of Mary to the Christmas story.

At the moment that Mary gives birth to Jesus in Bethlehem we finally have the living evidence of the union between the human and the divine nature of Christ. Jesus' human mother points to his human nature, just as the virginal conception, which we have discussed in the previous chapter, confirms the divine. And while we acknowledge here once more the importance of the virginity of Mary, at Christmas we also remember that she was a mother as well.

Just as ordinary mothers often relive all those details of the day their children were born, we learn from the New Testament nativity stories that Mary did too. "But Mary kept all these things, pondering them in her heart." This sentence, repeated twice with only slight variation in the second chapter of Luke's gospel, has always fascinated me. It is as though suddenly we were no longer merely looking back with hindsight from the crucifixion and resurrection to the birth of Jesus but actually catching a glimpse of Mary, puzzled, worried, anxious, wondering as all mothers do about the future of her child.

It is difficult now to separate all the glitter of the modern Christmas from the birth of Jesus. Whichever interpretation we prefer—the manger, the grotto, the annex, the shepherds or the wise men—the circumstances of Christ's birth were not easy.

> A cold coming we had of it,
> Just the worst time of year
> For a journey, and such a long journey:
> The ways deep and the weather sharp,
> The very dead of winter.

T.S. Eliot's *Journey of the Magi* is far removed from the joy and cheer that we now associate with the Christmas season. It was tough going for the magi.

> At the end we preferred to travel all night,
> Sleeping in snatches,
> With the voices singing in our ears, saying
> That this was all folly.

It must have been harder still for Mary, struggling from Nazareth to Bethlehem with only Joseph to help. It was a lonely beginning leading to a lonely death.

> There was a Birth, certainly,
> We had evidence and no doubt. I had seen birth and death

But had thought they were different; this Birth was
Hard and bitter agony for us, like Death, our death.

Births, unlike marriages, are usually private affairs.
Even in the western world, where families are no longer as
close as they once were, female relations and friends turn
to one another before a birth. Whatever the modern techniques and fashions, birth is still a somewhat silent and
mysterious affair, talked about intensely with other
would-be mothers, shared with would-be grandmothers,
with only occasional concessions to the brave-faced
father.

The birth of Jesus was a very public occasion, as public as any royal birth. Taking the nativity narrative of
Matthew, with Joseph, Herod and the wise men, together
with the story in Luke of Mary and the shepherds, a large
number of people were witness to this historic event.
Right from the start, beginning with the bustle of his birth
and ending with her solitary vigil at the foot of his cross,
there was to be little peace for Mary.

Ever since I was a teenager, watching or taking part in
the annual nativity play, Mary has always had a special
place in my Christmases. Our school play was full of action. Figures came and went. Gabriel and accompanying
angels, Elizabeth, Zechariah, Herod, shepherds, Simeon,
Anna, Balthasar, Melchior and Gaspar all had their en-
trances and exits. But Mary, with Joseph silently at her
side, was ever present. Hers was a difficult part, and to be
selected to play it was a great honor. Mary had to be beautiful, regal, welcoming and understanding. If this were not
enough, she also had to have an excellent voice in order to
sing the Magnificat unaccompanied in the opening scene
—no mean task for a fifteen or sixteen year old. Each year
we would sit at the back of the school hall crossing our
fingers that her voice would not falter. For us Mary had to
be perfect, and in all those years she never failed.

The only thing that Mary didn't have to do in that

long-ago play was to handle a baby. It didn't dawn on us teenagers that Mary was also a mother. I don't think we even had a doll in the crib, just a bundle of blankets and cushions. Somehow it didn't register that all Jesus really needed at that moment of birth was food, warmth and his mother's love. It never occurred to us that Mary didn't have to be beautiful or hold the stage. Those were extra but not necessary qualities. All she had to do was love a helpless baby.

When our first child, a daughter, was born, one of the many things my mother gave me was a little book called "It Must Be Hard To Be a Mother." I treasure it still, and after all these years find it a magnificent description of motherhood. It was one of those delightful books which are ostensibly written for children but which only adults fully appreciate. About a little girl mothering her favorite teddies and dolls, its few pages, with their simple sketches and one-line captions, managed to describe all those anxieties and wonders of motherhood far better than any learned medical tome.

The physical struggle of mother and baby at birth—that miraculous event of nature which propels a new, unique human being out into the world complete with tiny nails, floppy legs, intricate ears, wobbly head and curled up toes—is only the beginning of the complex process of bonding between parent and child, a bonding to which the mother holds the key.

What mother, looking at her first-born child, has not felt a sudden agony of helplessness in front of this vulnerable and dependent bundle? Who has not experienced those moments of panic when the baby cries for no apparent reason or loses weight? Who has not been seized by the terror of the first fall, first illness, first disappearance, and felt as Mary must have felt when losing Jesus in the temple in Jerusalem? And what mother has not looked down at that tiny body in the cot and wondered by what grace of God she has been blessed with this child?

The road ahead is daunting for any mother, and Mary, gazing at the shepherds, receiving the wise men or hurried off to Egypt by Joseph to escape the anger of Herod, must certainly have pondered all these happenings as she looked down at the living face of their baby boy and wondered why she had been so blessed and how she would find the strength for the years ahead.

8

"Suffered Under Pontius Pilate"

S everal European languages talk about persons turning up unexpectedly "like Pontius Pilate in the Creed." Where Mary of Nazareth is the human witness to the virginal conception, the Roman governor of Judea from A.D. 26 to 36 testifies to the historical fact of Jesus' public life and death. Jesus is no shadowy, legendary figure, but every bit as solidly real as the coins Pilate minted, the inscription from ancient Palestine that bears Pilate's name, and the two first century Jewish writers (Philo and Josephus) who add to what we know from the gospels about the Roman governor under whom Jesus was put to death. The name of Pilate fixes the Jesus-story at a particular point and place in human history. For Christian faith what happened under Pontius Pilate revealed God and brought us salvation in a full and final way that we can never find elsewhere.

The name of Pilate indicates also the horrifying climax of Jesus' sufferings: his death by crucifixion.

The new Rite of Christian Initiation of Adults (RCIA) proposes a moving ceremony for starting their lengthy preparation for baptism. A priest traces the sign of the cross on their forehead, ears, eyes, lips, breast and shoulders. In the prayers which accompany this action the priest asks the candidates to receive the sign of the cross as an expression of Christ's loving and powerful solidarity with them.

The candidates may be male or female. They may be young, middle-aged or old. They come from different races, cultures and personal backgrounds. But they all have two things in common with Christ: bodies and sufferings. In that RCIA ceremony the candidates begin their preparation for baptism by placing under the sign of the cross two utterly basic elements in their human condition: their bodies and their sufferings.

Our sufferings (which are always in one way or another connected with our bodies) thrust a great challenge at us. Are we willing to set them alongside Jesus in his passion? His cross was not an isolated cross; he died between two other men. Those two others crucified with him represent the whole history of human suffering. According to St. Luke, one criminal turned to our Lord with a prayer ("Jesus, remember me when you come into your kingdom"). The other criminal taunted Jesus (Lk 23:39–43). That is our challenge when we suffer. Will we turn to our brother Jesus crucified alongside us?

Left to ourselves, we would not be inclined to seek and find the crucified Jesus in our sufferings. And yet the whole human passion is in a mysterious way an extension of his. In the classic phrase of Blaise Pascal, "Jesus will be in agony to the end of the world. We must not sleep during that time." All that we suffer puts us in a special solidarity with the crucified Son of Man. Yet it can be hard, even extremely hard, to recognize Jesus in the darkness of our suffering and acknowledge that our agony is, mysteriously, an extension of his.

At times we suffer precisely because we try to follow Jesus. At other times our own mistakes and sins can bring us pain and anguish. Or else like Job we may suffer because of things that simply happen to us. All of these situations are covered by the invitation: "If any man wishes to come after me, let him take up his cross and follow me" (Mk 8:34).

Not "my cross" but "his cross." Pain is always personal. Certainly Jesus experienced an exceptionally cruel and ugly death. Like other victims of the Roman army of occupation in ancient Palestine, he was pinned up on a cross and writhed for hours in extreme pain before he expired. Nevertheless, there were limits to what he suffered on Calvary and had suffered before. He never knew the terrible hurt of a broken marriage or the agony of a drawn-out terminal disease. He never suffered as millions do under the burden of old age. As with everything else, Jesus' suffering was personal to him.

What happens to us if we do say "yes" to the particular crucifixion which comes to us? We will find that suffering accepted with Christ proves transforming. We will repeat the experience of St. Paul who came to know the mysterious truth that "when I am weak, then I am strong" (2 Cor 12:10). The apostle found power in the woundedness of his wandering life. He experienced the truth of Christ's words: "My grace is all you need, for my power comes to its full strength in weakness" (2 Cor 12:9).

Let me hasten to add here that I am not just repeating in a theoretical way some piece of teaching from the New Testament. Over and over again people in movements like Alcoholics Anonymous find "power coming to them in their weakness" (2 Cor 12:9).

In 1984 I attended a convention at the Sanctuary of Merciful Love, a huge and remarkable house of prayer fifty miles north of Rome. The center owes its existence to an utterly uneducated and extraordinarily holy Spanish nun, Madre Speranza (Mother Hope), who died in 1983. The closest town, Todi, crowns a nearby hill and has preserved three sets of walls: the Etruscan, the Roman and the medieval.

Not long before she died, Madre Speranza looked up the valley one evening at the lights of Todi and remarked: "How beautiful!" She paused and then said: "But behind every light there is a cross." She made me think of the greatest citizen of that charming town, Jacopone da Todi

(1230–1307). His life changed in 1268 when his wife was killed in a tragic accident. From his subsequent years as a Franciscan lay brother, Jacopone has left us many deeply devotional poems including the exquisite *Stabat Mater* ("At the cross her station keeping"). He accepted his suffering and did not curse God because of it. During Lent and Holy Week many of us sing Jacopone's *Stabat Mater*, a hymn which praises the Virgin Mary for the way she said "yes" to the terrible pain of her Son's passion and death.

On Good Friday around the world millions of believers venerate the cross and kiss the feet of the crucified Jesus. In my work as a priest it is one of the most moving moments in the whole year. Men and women, the young and the old, the sick, the sinful and the sorrowful, walk up with the burden of their lives. On their faces you can see what they are doing in joining their crucifixions to his.

I shrink from giving the impression of glorifying pain and wallowing in suffering. But "he suffered under Pontius Pilate" applies to all of us. There is always some Pontius Pilate around to put pain into our lives. No matter who we are, we cannot avoid the cross. The choice is simple. We can curse the pain. Or we can lay it at the feet of Jesus. If we do that, we will know our pain and our lives to be transformed.

Teaching in Rome from 1974 I lived through those years when various terrorist organizations carried out a whole series of senseless and cruel killings. At the same time, the funeral services of the victims over and over again showed how the grief-stricken relatives were ready to take their suffering to the crucified Jesus.

At the 1980 funeral of Walter Tobagi, a young journalist assassinated by terrorists in revenge for what he had written about them, Archbishop (now Cardinal) Carlo Martini spoke of the "mystery of meaninglessness and madness." But then he reminded the congregation of that great "certainty" to be found in the New Testament: "What is meaningless can gain a meaning." The prayers of the faithful which followed Archbishop Martini's homily showed most movingly how the crucified Jesus can bring those in terrible sorrow to see and affirm some meaning in what they experience. Stella Tobagi, left widowed with her two little children, had written the first prayer, and sat with her arms around her son and daughter while her sister read it:

Lord, we pray for those who killed Walter, and for all people who wrongly hold that violence is the only way for resolving problems. May the power of your Spirit change the hearts of men, and out of Walter's death may there be born a hope which the force of arms will never be able to defeat.

Murder or some other fierce tragedy can unexpectedly bring the cross into our lives. Or else our particular Pontius Pilate may turn up in a less dramatic fashion. Either way we all constantly face the challenge: Do we keep our eyes down and curse our cross? Or do we lift our gaze and link our pain with our unique fellow sufferer, the Son of God himself?

As you drive north from Italy into Austria, the character of the wayside shrines begins to change. Gradually the figure of the Virgin Mary gives way to Christ crucified. Finally Mary disappears almost entirely, to be found, if at all, in lonely vigil at the foot of the cross.

We happened to make this journey one Christmas. We left the colorful, bustling cribs which fill the churches in Rome and drove north into Austria for a holiday.

Surrounded by a happy, energetic family it is all too easy to forget that other side to Christmas, that heightened feeling of loneliness which comes to the ill or suffering or bereaved during the festivities.

In my own desire to make the most of the holidays I

left this present chapter behind to be completed on my return to Rome. "Not to be opened until the New Year" you had written thoughtfully across the envelope that you handed to me a few days before Christmas. I should have known better than to think that pain and suffering can be put away in a drawer until it is convenient.

Across the border we found the crucifix. As we waited for the start of the Christmas midnight mass in the cold of the darkened, silent and unusually austere Austrian church, the one point of light in the building was focused on the figure of Christ on the cross. The Christ child behind the altar was only lit much later. Then, mass over, back in our warm and friendly hotel, my brother's account of the death of a friend's daughter mingled with the noise of our excited children as they waited for their presents.

She died just before Christmas after a six year struggle with Hodgkin's disease. At the outset she was told that she had a ninety-five percent chance of recovery. Five years into her suffering her family was told that she wouldn't see another Christmas. The family packed and went on holiday to Florence. She lived through that Christmas. Told again the following year that she wouldn't see another Christmas, she and her mother set off that autumn for Rome. It seems to have been a happy, busy holiday, but this time the doctors were right. On December 13, her saint's day, she seemed somewhat better as her mother helped her to get ready for bed. That night she died at the age of twenty-two, after six progressively agonizing years of illness.

It was not only a story of suffering my brother told among the clatter of Christmas. It was above all an account of the Christian faith and serenity of this stricken family throughout those years. It was the strength of their belief which shone out on that Christmas night the daughter didn't live to see.

I never knew her and I shall probably never know her parents. Sadly she will never know how many people her faith has touched. Along with Madre Speranza we mourn for the suffering behind those lights on the hills. But the light on the cross of suffering can and does spark new hope in unexpected places.

As inexplicable as it seems to non-Christians, the concept of suffering is fundamental to an understanding of the Christian way of life. Had Christ died peacefully in old age and then risen from the dead, Christianity would be as different as if Christ had died horribly and then never been seen again. The resurrection without the crucifixion would have been as incomplete as the crucifixion without the resurrection.

In this part of the Creed, however, we are not just called on to confront suffering. The Creed might easily have read: "suffered, was crucified, died and was buried." For the writers of the Creed this was not enough. The figure of Pontius Pilate was important.

It is of course very comforting to come finally to someone we can demonstrate existed. To be able to date the death of Christ from the governorship of Pontius Pilate is a great relief in moments of shaky faith. We all long to have provable facts on which to base our belief. However, the writers of the early Creed may have singled out Pilate for an additional reason. Memories of Rome's persecution of the Christians were still vivid in the second century when in any case the persecution continued. Pilate, a Roman, must therefore have been a perfect symbol of all that the followers of Christ dreaded most. Finally, on a more mundane level, straight common sense tells us that the man who signs a death warrant is responsible for the victim's suffering.

However, in the aftermath of repeated twentieth century atrocities, particularly the Jewish holocaust, the boundaries of individual responsibility for human suffering have been extended further than ever before. In moral, if not necessarily legal, terms it is no longer just the official who puts his signature to the order whom we accuse of torture, persecution or death, but also all those along the line involved in the deed.

Should we therefore throw all the blame for Christ's suffering at Pilate? A weak man used his official power for political ends to rid himself of an awkward but innocent victim. But who of those involved in bringing Christ to the cross was not morally weak: Judas, Caiaphas, Annas, Herod, Peter? Who stood up for the innocent victim? How many of us are not weak when it comes to taking up our cross to follow Christ?

Should we even try to find a scapegoat to blame for Christ's sufferings? For centuries Christians have looked elsewhere for the culprits of Christ's death, accusing first the Romans and then the Jews of the deed, with the subsequent devastating effects we all know. To blame others is to shift the responsibility from ourselves. Weren't the followers of Jesus as responsible as his enemies were for his sufferings in those hours which led to the crucifixion?

It is one of our most basic instincts to blame on others what goes wrong and to claim for ourselves what goes right. We constantly find excuses for our shortcomings. "I didn't have time," "I wasn't there," "I didn't know," are all phrases as old as Adam's: "The woman whom thou gavest to be with me, she gave me of the fruit of the tree, and I ate." We, like Adam, will blame God or someone else for our difficulties if we possibly can.

Our sufferings are Christ's sufferings, but Pilate's actions are our actions. All of us could, maybe have and probably will act with the moral weakness of Pilate some time in our lives. We shall certainly cause others suffering, possibly willingly and intentionally, probably unwillingly and unintentionally. Often we bury ourselves in our own sufferings or blame others for an injustice done. How often do we admit to the sufferings we cause and accept the blame?

9

"Crucified, Died and Was Buried"

Recently I was writing a long article on crucifixion for a biblical dictionary. This meant revisiting what authors around the time of Jesus had to say about that atrociously cruel form of execution. The Jewish writer Josephus witnessed hundreds of men dying on crosses during the siege of Jerusalem. He called crucifixion "the most wretched of deaths."

Normally the ancient sources were reluctant to describe any crucifixion in much detail. It was such a painful and utterly shameful way of dying. The Romans used it regularly to preserve law and order against troublesome criminals, slaves and rebels. In Palestine crucifixion was a public reminder of Jewish servitude to a foreign power.

St. Paul did not exaggerate when he called the crucified Jesus "a stumbling block to the Jews" and "folly" to others (1 Cor 1:23). Nothing in the Old Testament suggests that the messiah could suffer such a fate. On the contrary, a crucified person, so far from being sent by God to redeem us, was understood to be cursed by God (Gal 3:13). For non-believers it seemed "sheer folly" (1 Cor 1:18) to proclaim that the crucified Jesus was the Son of God and divine Lord of the world. The extreme dishonor of his dying on a cross counted against any such claims.

What sense can we find in Jesus ending up in that

horrible way? What did his crucifixion mean? Why did he die on the cross?

One straightforward answer is that we, his brothers and sisters, killed him. He was simply too good for us. His being there was an embarrassment, a reproach to us. He set the standard altogether too high. He said so many impossible things about blessing those who curse us, about pardoning people seventy times seven times, about giving God everything and holding nothing back. Our hatred boiled up against him and we hurried him off to the cross.

In his suffering Jesus stood alone against our malice. According to the gospel stories of the passion, no one spoke up for him except the wife of Pontius Pilate and the good thief. No one lifted a finger to help him. We wanted him out of the way. Three men stood in for us and did the deed: a Roman governor, a Jewish priest and a disciple of Jesus. Through Pilate's weakness, Caiaphas' sense of expediency and Judas' treachery it was done.

The disturbing reproaches of the Good Friday liturgy ("My people, what have I done to you? How have I offended you?") imply that we are all spiritually connected with Pilate, Caiaphas and Judas. These men played out a drama in which we can recognize our sins of self-concern, greed and readiness to misuse power. We have no in-built guarantee that we could never be just as ruthless, treacherous and uncaring. Of course, each of us has no conscience to examine but his or her own. But do I find in myself weaknesses that—given the required circumstances—would even make me join forces with those who directly killed Jesus? If I do, am I willing to "accept the blame," as was said at the end of the last chapter?

Yet, is the whole history about our honestly accepting the blame? If the crucifixion were merely the result of our weakness, treachery and hatred, it would be enough to make us despair of ourselves and the whole human race. We could only wring our hands and say: "Yes, we once had the Son of God with us, but we hated him so much that we crucified him." We could only break down and weep bitterly as St. Peter did, or else come back from Calvary beating our breasts for shame and sorrow (Lk 23:48) over the "most wretched of deaths" by which we eliminated Jesus. That is our side of the story. But God's side of the story is far more important. It is that which gives deep meaning to Calvary and saves us from disillusionment and despair.

For one thing, Christ's death revealed how far his love for us could go: "Having always loved his own who were in the world," at the end "he showed the full extent of his love" (Jn 13:1). During his ministry he had tried to persuade us that he truly loved us. "Come to me, all whose work is hard, whose load is heavy; and I will give you relief" (Mt 11:28). He wept over God's city and cried out, "O Jerusalem, Jerusalem. How often have I longed to gather your children, as a hen gathers her brood under her wings, but you would not let me" (Lk 13:34). John's gospel tells us of the beautiful promise, "the bread which I will give is my own flesh for the life of the world" (Jn 6:51), and describes the sad reaction: "Many of his disciples exclaimed: this is more than we can stomach! Why listen to such talk?" (Jn 6:60). Later in the same gospel Caiaphas responds to the raising of Lazarus by declaring it to be in the national interest that Jesus die (Jn 11:50).

It takes a lot to change our hearts and persuade us. For every generation Christ's arms opened wide on the cross remain a compelling gesture of love. Who is more helpless and vulnerable than a man pinned to a cross and left to die slowly? It was love which made Jesus that helpless and that vulnerable.

In the town of Würzburg in West Germany I once saw a crucifix which made me think: "The artist lacked good taste to produce a work like that. The parish priest showed no common sense in putting it in his church." The arms of the crucified Jesus had come away from the cross. Huge nails pierced the two hands which were held out in a gesture of appeal to the worshipers. But then I reflected:

"The love that stopped Jesus from running away and led him to accept the cross went far beyond common sense. Good taste alone would never have carried Jesus through his ministry, even less have brought him to Calvary."

John's gospel speaks of the love revealed in the crucifixion (Jn 15:13). It knows too the power of that death to reverse the thrust of sin and "gather into one the children of God who had been scattered" (Jn 11:52). From the beginning of the human story sin has been at work, dividing us from one another and setting us against God. Cain cuts himself off from his family by murdering his brother Abel. St. Peter moves away from Jesus by denying that he ever knew him. All sin is like that—divisive and separating. From the cross, however, came a love which mysteriously burned away barriers and divisions. People began to gather together at the feet of the crucified Jesus: his mother Mary, the beloved disciple, Mary Magdalene, Joseph of Arimathea and the rest. This little group of men and women grew to be a vast army. On Good Friday millions of people walk up together to kneel and kiss Christ's wounded feet. In that part of the Holy Week services we see right before our eyes how his death continues to "gather into one the children of God who have been scattered."

Four hundred years before Christ, the Greek philosopher Plato suggested the kind of fate that a perfectly just person could expect: "The just man, as we have pictured him, will be scourged, tortured and imprisoned. His eyes will be put out, and after enduring every humiliation he will be crucified." Christians found this passage in the *Republic* to be a remarkable pagan prophecy of what happened to Jesus himself.

What Christians did not always fully appreciate, however, was the difference between Plato's "perfectly just" person and that perfectly loving person, Jesus. Plato was right about what society does, with depressing frequency, to uncompromisingly just and good individuals. But Jesus was much more than Plato's perfectly just person appearing on the human scene. He was love personified. His human and divine love made Jesus vulnerable in the extreme.

As regards Jesus' death, St. Paul never mentions the betrayal by Judas, the flight of the other male disciples, the legal proceedings before the religious authorities and Pilate, and the place of execution. He remains silent about the conflicts aroused during the ministry, the groups and individuals who emerged to menace Jesus, and the attempts made on his life before the end finally came on Calvary. One thing blots out everything else for Paul—the crucifixion itself. His concentration on the way Jesus died lets all the surrounding historical detail slip out of the picture. When he angrily demands "Was Paul crucified for you?" (1 Cor 1:13), it is like someone today saying about a friend: "He died in the electric chair," or "They stood him against a wall and drove a car at him." The sheer horror pushes other considerations away. One does not need to explain who "they" were, or why he died in the electric chair. Likewise the mere fact that Jesus died by crucifixion fills Paul's mind and provides more than enough material for thought.

As well as anything else he wrote about the crucifixion, Paul's letter to the Galatians caught the horror of that death in which Jesus seemed like one cursed by God (Gal 3:13). But that same letter also signaled the apostle's new basis for life: "I live by faith in the Son of God, who loved me and gave himself for me" (Gal 2:20).

To be sure, from the time of the New Testament Christians have found various ways of making sense of Jesus' ugly, painful and humiliating death. Yet the supreme clue to Calvary is love—not some softly sentimental love but a love that can move and change human hearts in a world where true caring and real compassion seem at times like a lost art.

Dante closed the *Divine Comedy* with his words about

"the love that moves the sun and the other stars." If Jesus' crucifixion is not to stop our mind cold with its leisurely cruelty, we need to recall his utterly self-giving love that turns this "most wretched of deaths" into the means for creating a new world and a new humanity. It is the love of the crucified Jesus which lets us see that our existence is not a tragic tale told by a fool, but one that promises a happy homecoming. In Dante's bold terms, the love dramatized on Calvary changes a human tragedy into a divine comedy.

F or a while in my teens I worked as a volunteer in an American military hospital somewhere in Pennsylvania. My dreams of becoming a twentieth century Florence Nightingale were short-lived. After a few visits I knew that if I saw any more mangled limbs, unhealed wounds, vacant expressions, decaying bodies, or blown-away faces, or smelled any more stinking urine bags, I would vomit. I turned my back and fled, not quite literally, but almost.

Today there is no longer any stench, nausea, shame or fear about the crucifixion. Twentieth century torturers have invented even more revolting ways to keep their fellows alive while slowly putting them to death. And the cross, once so ghastly a reality that it did not emerge as a symbol of Christianity for several centuries, has long become a glorious part of our cultural heritage. We gild it, bejewel it, carve it, mold it, paint it, wear it. We see it in a multitude of ways and often live in danger of not seeing it at all. Only occasionally do we see a crucifix which brings us up short or read a description of a crucifixion which sets our stomach heaving. If we sometimes find it hard to relive all the physical suffering of the cross, we find it even harder to understand the shame which was once attached to the way Christ died.

In this scientific age it is perhaps that science-defying

event, the resurrection, which is one of the main stumbling blocks to belief in Christianity. In the time of Jesus it was the crucifixion. To put it another way: A Jewish contemporary of Christ might possibly have expected him to rise again from the dead. There was something miraculous and superhuman in this. But how could he believe in a man put to death so humiliatingly, publicly and shamefully? How could this human hung between two thieves, unable to defend himself let alone others from Romans, naked, in mortal and physical agony, heaved down from the cross as dead as any other, be the messiah? Only Christ's closest followers could have been partly prepared for this.

At that moment, before the resurrection, everything must have seemed lost. It is easy for us and even for the writers of the New Testament to look back from the resurrection and understand the significance of the crucifixion. With hindsight, the prophecies of the Old Testament about the messiah take on their right significance, and even Christ's own words have new meaning. But in the hours of the crucifixion and its immediate aftermath there was no hindsight. There was one brutal fact: a dying, then a dead body, to be buried hastily before the sabbath in a borrowed tomb.

In order to understand what those moments must have been like, we have to cut ourselves off from all that we as privileged believers know came next, and imagine that the Creed stops here.

Perhaps we can come close to what Jesus' followers felt if we think of our own experience of death, particularly of the death of a young person with a seemingly wonderful life ahead. Faith in the goodness of life, which was just beginning to grow as we watched this person live, is suddenly shaken by an unexpected and totally unmerited death. We are caught unaware, and what seemed to make sense doesn't make sense any longer. The greater our expectations, the greater our sense of despair, injustice, disorientation and frustration.

However much we as Christians believe in a life after death, at that precise moment of death we are devastated by the cold reality of an indefinite separation from the person we love. We find relief in doing the best we can—a moving funeral, an appropriately magnificent monument, the gathering of friends. We hang on to earthly things in our separation and say goodbye as best we can.

Mourning is a vital part of death. Those who for some reason have no body to mourn—families of soldiers missing in action, mothers who miscarry during pregnancy—are known to feel the desolation of death longer than others. Even small children need to mourn in order to show their love and understanding. Once I made the mistake of removing the remains of a family pet before the children came home from school. The tears at the animal's death were nothing compared to the enduring suspicion that I had not treated the unfortunate corpse with due respect.

It was concern for the body which took Mary Magdalene to the tomb the day after the sabbath. It was her desperation at the discovery that the body was gone which found her weeping at the tomb and saying to the man she mistook for the gardener: "Sir, if you have carried him away, tell me where you have laid him, and I will take him away" (Jn 20:15).

The empty tomb was no less devastating to her than it would be to us if the body of a loved one disappeared. At that precise moment the fact that Jesus' body had gone was of supreme importance to his mourners.

A body and a grave helps us to bridge the separation of death, to heal those feelings of remorse for sentences left unsaid, actions incompleted, resolutions unfulfilled, questions unasked, moments not lived to the full, love cut short.

The followers of Christ must have felt all this and more in those days of death. Had their master led them all this way to leave them like this? We, with the comfort of hindsight, have the resurrection ahead of us. We know the happy ending—as we live through the suffering of Christ or face the death of those we love. They had no clear idea what would happen next.

It could not have been easy to follow Jesus to his tomb. It must have taken considerable courage to conquer the fear of the Romans, the bloodthirsty jeering of the mob, the nauseating spectacle of the crucifixion, and to stand almost alone to watch a man you loved tortured to death.

Perhaps it was faith which found them there. I doubt whether it was hope. My own feeling is that it was neither faith nor hope but that profound love described by St. Paul which found that small band of women and one or two men with Christ at the foot of the cross. "Love bears all things, believes all things, hopes all things, endures all things" (1 Cor 13:7).

10

"He Descended to the Dead"

L ast year just before All Souls Day two friends from Cremona drove me west across the Lombardy plain to Mantua. Before leaving town they pointed out the school where the greatest Latin poet had studied. "Virgil was born near Mantua, but went to school in Cremona," they proudly announced. We stopped to see an exhibition of photographs showing how ugly apartment blocks had been steadily engulfing agricultural land and old farmhouses that still ring Cremona.

A gray sky hung low over the fields. At the end of a particularly warm October the temperature had suddenly dropped. The leaves were starting to fall from the trees that lined the road. Shortly before Mantua heavy traffic outside a huge cemetery slowed us down. Along the road florists were doing a brisk trade selling pots of bright chrysanthemums. The license plates on the cars showed just how many people had come back from distant cities to grieve, pray and leave flowers at the graves of their dear departed.

In Mantua we spent hours being guided around the faded magnificence of the endless Gonzaga palace. After the terrible sack of 1630 the city never recovered its former grandeur. In 1708 the last duke died in exile. The family had come to power and wealth in the fourteenth century. Today the name "Gonzaga" does not even appear in Mantua's telephone book. It is almost as if the glory of the Gonzagas had never been—that the dukes, the artists, the cardinals and St. Aloysius Gonzaga were little more than figments of our historical imagination, mere flotsam swept away on the racing waters of time.

On the way back to Cremona I quoted Virgil's melancholy summary of our condition: "*Sunt lacrimae rerum et mentem mortalia tangunt*" (which one can roughly translate as "there are tears at the heart of things and our mortal condition touches the heart").

"But there's bread under the snow," commented Mimma. "What do you mean by that?" I asked. "It's a proverb from the farming community," she explained. "They work the fields and sow the seed now—before the feast of St. Martin on November 11. The earth keeps its basic heat. The snow isn't violent. The seed germinates. When the blanket of snow disappears, up pop the green sprouts."

That day in Lombardy set me thinking about a third element in Christ's radical solidarity with us. He stands with us not only through having a body and sufferings but also through the place where bodily suffering eventually takes us all, death itself. At the end he matches our common fate by descending to the dead.

From the beginning of Christianity there have been those who could not stomach the fact that Jesus truly died. Some early Gnostics, for example, claimed that only an image hung on the cross. The real Christ escaped to live and laugh over the deception practiced on his enemies.

But Christian believers and, indeed, historians know otherwise: Jesus truly died. His story reflects our lives, and our end when we cave in and die.

The sights on the road between Cremona and Mantua vividly imaged for me our common mortality. The grain and grapes had been harvested. The days were shortening, the leaves were falling, there was a feel of snow in the air. Life was closing down. The only flowers within sight were those the Italians generally reserve for their cemeteries and their dead.

As much as any of the gospel writers, Mark reveals a strong sense of Jesus being on the road to crucifixion and a descent to the dead. The way of the cross emerges clearly when Jesus moves from Caesarea Philippi, through Galilee, on to the regions of Judea and Transjordan, and finally takes the road going up to Jerusalem (Mk 8:27–10:53). During this pilgrimage from the green and fertile north to the stony and harsh south, Jesus three times announces his violent death and invites his close followers to become cross-bearers with him (Mk 8:34). The healing of a blind beggar strikingly symbolizes how the disciples have to be taught to see what life with Jesus involves. Bartimaeus receives his sight and becomes the only person cured by Jesus in Mark's story to go on and follow the Lord (Mk 10:46–53). Miraculously enabled to see, he can follow Jesus "on the road" going up to Jerusalem and death.

Most likely Mark consciously intended the pattern of teaching about the cross that emerges from chapters 8, 9 and 10. One pattern which he almost certainly did not intend but which nevertheless we find in his text suggests a progressive restriction that reaches its climax with the crucifixion and burial. Jesus is taken from Gethsemane to the high priest's house, and from there to Pilate's palace and eventually "the place of the skull" (Mk 15:22). Things narrow down and space closes in, as we move from a garden, through buildings, to Golgotha, "the place of the skull," and the tomb cut out of rock (Mk 15:46). The scenes named as the passion story unfolds convey a sense of a world limiting Jesus ever more until finally his corpse is buried beneath the rock.

The "descent to the dead" reminds us, if we need that reminder, that Jesus truly died; his human story came to a dead stop. But this article of the Creed also indicates his solidarity with all men and women, of all places and times.

95

The fact that he died not alone but between two others visibly and publicly drew him into the circle of mortality —with all those who will ever live and die, including those who lived before him and those who have lived after him without ever hearing his name.

Christian faith professes, however, that Jesus not only died *with* all others but also *for* all others and to their advantage. A Chinese proverb declares: "The right man sitting in his house thinking the right thought will be heard five hundred miles away." Likewise, if we dare put it this way, the right man hanging on the cross for the right cause will save human beings from one end of history to the other. The inter-connectedness of all things is an old truth. The new Christian claim is that for their everlasting benefit all human beings and their world are inter-connected with a particular "descent to the dead" that took place two thousand years ago just outside Jerusalem.

One way of elucidating the universal consequences of this particular death is to point to Jesus' personal identity. It was not just some very noble individual who descended to the dead, but God's only Son who had come among us. The God of all the world was personally involved in Jesus' crucifixion. Could the Son of God live and die and yet fail to transform the nature of human life and death—for all of us and for all time? One who was and is truly and fully divine experienced "from the inside" what it is to live and die. That descent from life into death on the part of God's Son meant changing the common destiny of us all.

Another perspective on Jesus' death recalls that as it issues into his resurrection, he initiates the end of all history. Through the death and resurrection of Jesus the close of the whole human story has already flared forth. The fate that swept him from the visible scene made him the first to enter into that final state to which all human beings are called through him.

However we verbally express the universal impact of

Jesus' descent to the dead, we should not lay aside the role here of Christian art. In *The Black Prince* the novelist Iris Murdoch claims that "art . . . is the telling of truth, and is the only available method for the telling of certain truths." Admittedly, art has not been the only available method for telling the truth about Christ. Otherwise, the gospel writers, for example, would never have been inspired to set down in writing what Jesus' followers had "heard with their ears, seen with their eyes, looked upon and touched with their hands" (1 Jn 1:1). Nevertheless, Christian art has consistently mirrored with a peculiar intensity and expressed with a special success the essential items of our faith. Apropos of the belief we are considering, representations of Jesus' descent to the dead, especially eastern icons, tell the truth about the significance of his death for all humanity. In those representations he often appears delivering Adam and Eve from the realm of the dead—a powerful symbol of the universal impact of what happened in Jesus' dying and rising.

The best day for prayerfully mulling over Christ's descent to the dead is undoubtedly Holy Saturday, a privileged moment when we can look in two directions. We look back to Good Friday when death engulfed and devoured Jesus. In a way that goes far beyond Virgil's melancholy summing up of our human condition, the passion story shows us that "there are tears at the heart of things." On the first Good Friday nearly two thousand years ago a few women weeping at the place of the skull were at the painful heart of things.

When, however, we face in the other direction on Holy Saturday, we know that it is not enough simply to take winter, pain and death for granted. The Gonzagas are gone from Mantua but one of their sons provides the name for thriving educational institutions around the world. Jesus died and was buried under the rock. But there is bread under the snow and new life rising from the tomb.

97

Jesus descended to the dead but he also rose to full and final glory. Ultimately it is his resurrection that can answer Virgil's sorrowful lines.

I f art is the telling of truths, then it would seem that we as Christians still have enormous problems with death. Images of death in western culture, even quite modern ones, are not comforting. We are confronted by hooded fellows with scythes, avenging angels, skulls, fire and torment. Death is considered dark, shadowy, cold and, to quote John Donne, "dost with poison and sickness dwell." To borrow from T.S. Eliot's "Whispers of Immortality," which was written three centuries after Donne's "Divine Meditations," we, like Webster, are much possessed by death, by the skull beneath the skin, the hopeless grin and daffodil bulbs pushing their way through the sockets where the eyes once were.

Funerals for the most part are not only sad occasions, which would be natural enough, but are downright depressing affairs, with the mourners dressed in black and the organist compelled to play slow, solemn music. It is rare that we leave a funeral at peace with ourselves and our maker, giving thanks for a life completed, content in the knowledge that "Death is but the blowing out of the candle at the break of dawn."

I heard this glorious and comforting description once during a Sunday homily and I have seen it since on a funeral card. But it is relatively unknown and I have been unable to trace its origin.

Somewhere down the centuries a gap has opened up between what we profess to believe as Christians and what we actually think will happen at death. So often human life is not lived as one part of a whole but as an end in itself. In the gospels the death of Jesus is a short interlude between dying—so often confused with death itself—and rising again. It is a transitory period between one type of existence (earthly) and another (heavenly)—from the small candle to the great dawn.

In contrast to this Christian message, death has come to be looked on as the opposite of life rather than its progression. We seem to find death no less terrifying now than we did before the death of Christ on the cross. We tend to lose sight of the message that it is in death that we shall discover the real meaning of our earthly lives. We see it is an end rather than a new beginning.

We may not worry too much these days about hell fire and ghastly torments for the "undeserving" after death. But we fear death no less, and try to push it out of the way into an unobserved corner of the hospital or clinic. Not many people are lucky enough to die in the peace of their homes today. Lest it disturb the sensibility of the living, death goes out through the back door into the cemetery or the flames of the crematorium. Modern death has become as antiseptic, streamlined, packaged and expensive as many other aspects of our consumer society.

Very broadly speaking, societies which place a high value on the life of the individual are the ones which find it particularly difficult to cope with death. Ironically, it is partly the value we as Christians put on individual, human existence which makes death difficult to face. Our moral code centers on preserving human life from its very origins to its final, unprovoked end. This has led to wonders of modern science and medicine, but it also gives rise to a feeling of defeat and helplessness when death finally takes over. Death is interpreted as a failure of our human powers, the point where we are forced to give up.

Whatever amazing techniques we shall be able to use to expand human life in the future, when transplants, genetic engineering and other science-fiction techniques become everyday reality, we shall not be able to put off death forever. But would we really want our lives to go on indefinitely? It is a sobering but perhaps comforting thought that while we have perfected ways to control numerous aspects of our life by preventing it, piloting it, prolonging it or curtailing it, we have no real power over death at all.

We do not even have a way of imagining what death is really like. We hang on to tales of people who have "come back from the dead," clinically speaking, but we know that these cannot be reliable guidelines. Even the gospels which give us descriptions of Christ's life, crucifixion and resurrection appearances give us nothing directly on the mystery of death. In all four gospel stories we are led straight from the burial of Jesus to the discovery of the empty tomb.

So far in these chapters we have passed through faith, creation, life and suffering, which in some way we can measure against our own direct experience and reason. In many of the following chapters, on judgment, the Holy Spirit and the forgiveness of sins, we can rely on eye-witness accounts or write from our own experience. But in front of death we are faced with the great unknown, armed not with experience or reason but with the belief based on trust that Jesus Christ has gone before us not only through life but also through death. In front of death we are forced to trust what we reasonably believe to be true.

When we were kids we were led to believe that if we learned to swim, then no harm would come to us when we jumped off the top of the pier jutting out into one of the deep-water bays in the north of the island. Gradually we learned to swim, without much style or strength, our heads thrown back and with our noses held high out the water to avoid the waves.

Finally the day came when we were allowed to jump. The distance from the top of the granite pier to the water was terrifying, but there was no way back. Parents and friends were idly hanging on the railings to watch us go and others were pressing for their turn behind. Did we know enough to swim out of the plunge? Would we hit the rocks or get tangled in the mooring ropes tying the small fishing boats to the pier? Would some awful strand of sea-weed hold us down? Our fears were childish, but no less real for that. Not today, please, not today. Tomorrow would be much better. But it was too late. Out into the void we went and down into the deep sea, lungs aching, water burning up our nose and feet kicking frantically to bring us back to the surface. Those seconds seemed an eternity but the burst back into the air, the big welcome from the crowd on the pier and the overwhelming sense of a new freedom were worth every bit of our previous fear and panic.

What we did not know then and could only understand much later, when as parents ourselves we watched our children jump, was that the child's anxiety was a pale shadow of the parents' fear as the little body disappeared beneath the water. Nor could we know as we flung ourselves from the pier that we were only allowed to jump because there was no real risk ahead, and that had some unforeseen danger threatened, each parent would have sacrificed everything to save the child.

Like Jesus, we will come back from the waters of death. Both in life and in the descent to the dead, God will see to our safety.

11

"On the Third Day He Rose Again"

Christianity did not begin with some general religious message about God being the Father and Mother of us all. Nor did it begin with such a moral exhortation as "Let us love one another."

The Christian movement began with a thoroughly specific and astonishing factual claim about a particular person, Jesus of Nazareth. In utter disgrace he had died on a cross, crying out, "My God, my God, why have you forsaken me?"

Cicero, a Roman lawyer and statesman who died shortly before the birth of Jesus, called crucifixion "that most cruel and disgusting penalty." His fellow Romans frequently imposed this form of execution on slaves, violent criminals and rebels. The Dead Sea Scrolls and St. Paul show us that many people believed that God cursed those who died by crucifixion.

Yet shortly after Jesus' death and burial, St. Peter and others began claiming that he had risen from the dead and should be accepted as the messiah, Son of God and divine Lord of the universe. The evidence from 1 Corinthians 15:3–8, the book of Acts and elsewhere in the New Testament establishes that the preaching of the resurrection went back to the very origins of Christianity.

Both then and now Christian faith stands or falls with the resurrection of Jesus from the dead. It was this unique piece of good news which got Christianity going and keeps it going.

How did Peter, Paul and the others know that the unthinkable and the absurd had happened: a crucified and resurrected messiah? They did not directly witness the very event of the resurrection, but later they did see the risen Jesus himself. On a number of occasions he appeared to them. Secondly, his tomb was found to be open and empty.

What of us in the twentieth century? Why can we believe that the crucified Jesus rose from the dead? First, we have solid testimony coming to us from a number of men and women who launched Christianity. Jesus ended his earthly life nailed on a cross to die in slow agony. But then, some time afterward, he appeared gloriously alive to different individuals and groups of people, several hundred in all. St. Paul lists many of these witnesses. He adds his own testimony as a persecutor turned believer: "in the end he appeared also to me" (1 Cor 15:5–8).

At the same time, believing in the risen Christ is more than merely accepting the testimony of others to a unique event which took place nearly two thousand years ago. Easter faith means knowing the difference the living Jesus can make in our lives here and now. We experience his powerful presence in the scriptures and in the eucharist, but also in a thousand other ways. He comes to us in prayer, behind the faces of those who suffer and need our help, in the joys and pains of daily life.

Through the presence of the risen Jesus we can hope that our story will not end in the empty silence of annihilation. The world to which we go will be no gray haunt of ghosts, but a deeply satisfying existence in which we shall know our dear ones and be known by them. We have the promise, "If I go and prepare a place for you, I shall come again and take you to myself, so that where I am, you also may be" (Jn 14:3). In short, believing in Jesus' resurrection, we also hope for our own.

What was his resurrection like? It was no mere reanimation of his corpse. It was much more than his soul leaving the body and then coming back to it, like someone slipping out of a house at night and returning in the morning. St. Paul stresses the glorious transformation effected by resurrection (1 Cor 15:42ff). It means full and final freedom from suffering and death, and living an existence that rises above all the limits we now experience.

Luke and John also draw attention to the way the risen Lord has been changed and transformed. Closed doors are no obstacle to him (Jn 20:19, 26). He appears and disappears at will (Lk 24:31–36). People who have known him during his earthly existence fail, at least initially, to identify the risen Lord. On the road to Emmaus the two disciples recognize him only in the moment of his disappearance (Lk 24:31). Mary Magdalene at first supposes him to be a gardener (Jn 20:14f). Jesus has risen from the dead, and has become gloriously different.

Closely tied up with the nature of the bodily resurrection is the question of the empty tomb. Some Christians allege that faith in the risen Jesus does not need to affirm his empty tomb. He is himself risen from the dead, but his corpse decayed in the grave. "It would make no difference to my faith in his resurrection if the bones of Jesus were found." Over the years I have heard this statement from time to time, and it continues to bother me.

But why make a fuss? Surely I should be glad that the person in question believes in Jesus' personal resurrection? Provided Jesus lives a glorious, new life, does it really matter if the corpse laid in the tomb by Joseph of Arimathea quietly decomposed?

To begin with, those who summarily dismiss the empty tomb as unimportant normally do so in the name of "my faith." I have never heard any of them arguing that "it would make no difference to the church's faith in his resurrection if the bones of Jesus were found." I don't think they could argue that. One of the graffiti which turn up on walls in the spring shows what very many people would conclude if such a discovery were made: "There will be no Easter this year. They have found the body." This suggests how ordinary believers' faith in Jesus' resurrection does involve his grave being empty. They would not believe in his resurrection from the dead unless his tomb had been found open and empty. They take the empty tomb to be implied by what they confess in the Creed ("on the third day he rose again").

To judge from what I have heard ("It would make no difference to my faith . . ."), those who brush aside the empty tomb are not hoping to heighten thereby the quality of their Easter faith. They normally do not claim: "It would improve my faith if the bones of Jesus were found." What they are about seems rather to be an exercise in content reduction. How far can they go in reducing the content of faith and whittling away beliefs before their faith would collapse? What can be dropped without their suffering an essential loss?

Instead of calling this procedure "content reduction," one might speak of an "alternative scenario," a version of the Easter faith which tells of Jesus personally living in glory but shrugs off any questions about the fate of his crucified body. If the method of alternative scenarios works here, why not try it elsewhere? Would it really matter if he did not die on the cross but was taken down alive, recovered consciousness in the tomb, somehow got out, and so "appeared" alive to his disciples? Would it make no difference if the God of Jesus Christ was simply one and in no sense three?

I wonder about the usefulness, and indeed validity, of practicing this method of content reduction or alternative scenarios. People do not normally adopt this method in other areas of deep personal concern. At least so far no one has ever said to me, "It would make no difference to my life if my mother had a secret lover and my mother's husband was not my father." Most men and women accept trustingly that their mother's husband is their father and relate to him accordingly.

Something like this holds true of the Christian faith we have received through the community from the apostolic church. That original group of believers testified to the Son of God's personal resurrection, his empty tomb, his new existence with the Father and the sending of the Holy Spirit into our world. To accept such testimony in an attempt to understand it promises to be a more appropriate response than reducing the content of the New Testament's Easter message or imagining some alternative scenario which, for example, dropped the Holy Spirit from our account of God.

As regards the fate of Jesus' body, the gospels testify that Mary Magdalene (all four gospels) with one or more female companions (the gospels of Matthew, Mark and Luke) found his grave to be open and that the corpse had mysteriously disappeared.

There is a reasonable case to be made in support of the claim that Jesus' grave was discovered to be open and empty. Early arguments against the message of his resurrection seem to have admitted that his tomb was known to be empty. Naturally the opponents of the Christian movement explained away the missing body as a plain case of theft (Mt 28:11–15). But we have no early evidence that anyone, either Christian or non-Christian, ever alleged that Jesus' tomb contained his remains. Furthermore, it would have been impossible in Jerusalem for the disciples to start proclaiming his resurrection if his grave had not been empty. Their enemies could at once have produced his corpse to give the lie to that message.

These and further arguments support the historical conclusion that the tomb of Jesus was discovered to be empty. But the real challenge here is not to weigh the pros or cons of historical arguments. The challenge is to explore and appreciate what the empty tomb could and does mean. The right question is: "How would it improve our

Easter faith if we understood something of the empty tomb's significance?"

First of all, the emptiness of Jesus' grave reflects the holiness of what it once held, the corpse of the incarnate Son of God who lived for others and died to bring a new covenant of love for all people. This "holy one" could not "see corruption" (Acts 2:27). Second, the very emptiness of the tomb suggests and symbolizes the fullness of the new and everlasting life into which Jesus himself has gone. Graves naturally symbolize death and the end of life. The open and empty tomb of Jesus expresses the reversal of death and the start of a new life which will never end.

Third, the empty grave in Jerusalem says something vital about the nature of our redemption: that redemption is not a mere escape from our scene of suffering and death. Rather it means the transformation of this material, bodily world with its whole history of sin and suffering. The first Easter began the work of finally bringing our universe home to its ultimate destiny. God did not discard Jesus' earthly corpse, but mysteriously raised and transfigured it so as to reveal what lies ahead for human beings and their world. In short, the empty tomb is God's radical sign that redemption is not an escape to a better world but an extraordinary transformation of this world.

The Apostles' Creed sums up the essential scenario of Christianity. Admittedly in that prayer of faith we simply confess the crucified Jesus to be risen from the dead, without saying anything expressly about either his post-resurrection appearances or the discovery of his empty tomb. But it was through those appearances and that discovery that the first Christians came to know about his resurrection. There will be Easter again next spring because two thousand years ago they never found the body.

Early Christians knew that if they were wrong about Jesus' rising from the dead, they would be the "most pitiable" of all people (1 Cor 15:19). But they were not wrong. At the eucharist we can continue to cry out with joy: "Dying you destroyed our death, rising you restored our life. Lord Jesus, come in glory."

For an outsider to enter into the theological debate on the empty tomb would seem to be a clear case of fools rushing in where angels fear to tread. But in centuries past all kings had fools whose role it was not only to entertain the court but also to offer the king a different view on matters of state. Freed from the constraints of conventional wisdom and the restrictions of court etiquette, they were allowed liberties others were not permitted. Thanks to his very foolishness, the court jester could ramble where he pleased, safe in the knowledge that his speculations did not bear the same weight or consequence as those of others. It is therefore with the wisdom of fools that I approach the empty tomb.

"Why do you seek the living among the dead?" the angel asked the women who approached the tomb of Jesus that first Easter morning. Twenty centuries later we, like Mary Magdalene on that first Easter day, are still searching for the body to anoint in the tomb.

Even now we go back time and again in the hope of finding some bodily evidence for the life of Christ with which to end many of our doubts. Did Jesus really exist? Did he really live and die like other humans?

If we were to find a body, then a part of our faith would be made easier. Of course the Shroud of Turin would have been the perfect solution. If it had been the burial sheet of Christ, it would have given us the real image to which we could cling without all the difficulties created by the discovery of a body. To have been able to point to the shadow on the Shroud and say with reasonable certainty that that was the face of Christ would have been a wonderful comfort. But it was not to be.

So once again we are left staring at the empty tomb. As I have indicated in an earlier chapter, it is the resurrection which today presents would-be Christians and even Christians with their greatest difficulties. The crucifixion for the first followers of Christ was inconceivably shameful. For us the resurrection does not fit in with the patterns of twentieth century reason and scientific thought. It is not rational. It cannot be proved, and it is almost as confusing for us to think of a risen body as it was for Jews to ponder the messiah on a cross.

If anything, it would be easier for us to think of the risen Christ in a purely spiritual form, leaving behind a body to appear somewhat as a ghost might do. In this we are no different from the first Christians to whom Christ appeared. In Luke we read:

> As they were saying this, Jesus himself stood among them, and said to them: "Peace to you." But they were startled and frightened, and supposed that they saw a spirit. And he said to them, "Why are you troubled, and why do questionings rise in your hearts? See my hands and my feet, that it is I myself; handle me and see; for a spirit has not flesh and bones as you see that I have" (Lk 24:36–39).

We have been conditioned into dividing the body and the spirit, or soul, from one another. We generally think of the spirit separating from the body at death and going "somewhere else." We could in theory find the body of Jesus in the sepulchre and still have Easter. We could very comfortably believe in a spiritual resurrection. Must we really believe in a bodily one too?

For hundreds of years medicine has treated the body without considering the spirit or the mind. It is only comparatively recently, beginning perhaps with Freud, that the human being has come to be seen in its entirety, with the mind affecting the workings of the body and the well-being of the body linked inseparably to the functioning of the mind. It is only during recent decades that modern western medicine has come to treat the two—body and mind—in conjunction, having found it increasingly difficult to "cure" the body without treating the mind.

In many ways we are still suffering from centuries of conditioning in which the body played second place to the mind. In Victorian times, and even long before that, the body was the poor relation, the animal in us, the source of the unclean, the unmentionable and the uncontrolled, while the mind was the seat of the noble in us, the part which brought us nearer to the divine. For centuries we have divided our being in two. It is not that often that we give thanks for our bodies, those staggeringly magnificent and complex structures without which our earthly existence would be impossible.

At the heart of the Christian faith is the unification of the human and the divine in the body of Jesus Christ. But just as we may have trouble accepting the virginal conception, we also hesitate to believe in the empty tomb. We use a number of stratagems to justify our difficulties with the bodily resurrection of Christ: the writers of the gospels were conditioned by the appearances of Jesus when writing about the empty tomb; the resurrection language is inappropriate to describe what really happened; events were not really what we are told they were; body or no body, it does not make any difference anyway.

If on the other hand we see our bodies as a vital and essential part of our human existence, we may find it easier to be reconciled to the bodily resurrection of Christ. It seems strange to point to the body of Jesus as the vital evidence of his human nature during the period from his conception to his death, only to throw it out at the last moment as an unimportant part of the whole. If we are to reject the body of Jesus and leave it in the tomb as something of little importance, it is as though we were turning our backs on the human in Christ and settling only for the divine. If on the other hand we settle for a risen *body*, we find a part of the revolutionary message of the Christian faith. Christ did not duck out of the human condition at the last moment, leaving his body behind and divesting himself of his earthly self as though, mission completed, he could make a quick, convenient exit back to his divine home and abandon a set of useless bones. The earthly part of Jesus was not only *not* discarded but was considered of such importance that it was totally transformed, bodily remains and all, into a new whole.

In the resurrection, just as in the virginal conception, we have the perfect unity of the human body of Jesus with his divine nature. If we reject the virginal conception, we are rejecting a sign of the divine nature of Jesus in favor of the human. Likewise if we reject the bodily resurrection of Christ, we are rejecting a part of the human in favor of the divine.

As we stop to look into the empty tomb, we, like Mary Magdalene and the apostles, are afraid. We, like Mary Magdalene, ask where the body can be. We, like Mary, have fixed ideas about what we are looking for, and, unable to find it, we hesitate to accept the evidence before our eyes. We, like Mary, are so worried about the body that we fail to recognize what we are looking for when we see it before our eyes. We see the gardener, not the living Jesus. It is only through the intervention of Jesus that the truth is finally revealed. Jesus speaks to Mary in the garden. He talks to the disciples on the road to Emmaus. He invites Thomas to touch his scars.

Whatever interpretation we may care to put on the stories in the gospels, those to whom Jesus appeared were certain that there was no body in the sepulchre. It would seem reasonable to suppose that, human nature being what it is, Mary Magdalene would have searched to the end of her days for the body of Jesus had she not been satisfied that there was no body to find. Her meeting with Jesus in the garden put an end to her search forever. And if we, like Mary, are fortunate enough to meet Jesus in the garden, we shall know at last that we need never search the empty tomb again.

12

"He Ascended into Heaven"

The story of Christ's ascension at the beginning of the book of Acts can come across as embarrassingly mythological. Jesus takes off into the sky and disappears behind a cloud. Two angels in white robes show up and speak with one voice, telling the disciples not to stand around any more gazing open-mouthed into heaven. "This Jesus, who was taken away from you up into heaven, will come in the same way as you have seen him go" (Acts 1:11).

One turns with relief to the end of Luke's gospel where the same author reports in a much simpler way how the post-resurrection appearances to the original disciples ended. While blessing his disciples, the risen Jesus "parted from them" (Lk 24:51). At that point some ancient copies of the gospel add: "and was carried up into heaven." Even if those words actually come from Luke himself and are not added by a later hand, it is still a less vivid and embarrassing scenario than we find at the start of Acts. There are no angels and no cloud. If we agree with many scholars that the words "and was carried up into heaven" were slipped in by a later copyist, Luke's gospel does not speak at all of Jesus' going up into the sky.

In this way we can play the end of Luke's gospel off against the beginning of his Acts of the Apostles, so as to demythologize the vivid scenario of the ascension. This means underscoring the resurrection and downplaying the importance of the feast we celebrate between Easter and Pentecost.

After all, in the eucharistic acclamations that follow the consecration we say: "Dying you destroyed our death, rising you restored our life. Lord Jesus, come in glory." We do not say, "Ascending you restored our life." The fourth acclamation reads: "Lord, by your cross and resurrection you have set us free. You are the savior of the world." There is no talk about "your cross and ascension" setting us free.

Can we be satisfied with reducing the Ascension to the status of a minor feast, a small peak between the towering mountains of Easter and Pentecost? May we explain the ascension as the close of the risen Jesus' appearances to his original disciples and leave it at that?

This treatment of the ascension becomes more difficult, once we begin to notice other passages in the New Testament which speak of Jesus being "exalted to the right hand" of God the Father (Acts 2:33; see Acts 7:55–56; Rom 8:34; Col 3:1). In confessing that "he ascended into heaven and is seated at the right hand of the Father," the Creed reflects the biblical pictures of Jesus going up from our world to assume his rightful place alongside his heavenly Father.

One New Testament hymn speaks of Christ being "taken up in glory" (1 Tim 3:16). Another hymn expresses his exaltation in terms of his universal authority and divine identity being now revealed:

> God has highly exalted him
> and bestowed on him the name
> which is above every name,
> that at the name of Jesus
> every knee should bow,
> in heaven and on earth and under the earth,
> and every tongue confess
> that Jesus Christ is Lord,
> to the glory of God the Father (Phil 2:9–11).

The pictorial counterpart for this hymn which St. Paul quotes in his letter to the Philippians you can find in the twelfth century Church of St. Clement in Rome. When you enter from the street and stand in the aisle, you can lift your eyes high above the altar to a majestic mosaic. It represents Christ ruling in divine glory over the whole universe. At a lower level beneath your feet are the ruins of a fifth century church. You can go even further down to visit a first century alley and the traditional site of the home of St. Clement of Rome. From under the earth and on the street level this remarkable church invites visitors to look up at Christ surrounded by the stars of heaven and acknowledge him to be the glorious Lord of the whole world.

Unquestionably the early church speaks more of his resurrection than of his ascension when stating what happened to Christ himself after his death and burial. Nevertheless, the New Testament *does* talk of his going up into heaven. Christians are faithful to the scriptures when they follow up Easter by celebrating the feast of the Ascension. In the Creed they confess that Jesus not only "rose again" but also that he "ascended into heaven."

In what ways do these two beliefs relate to each other or else differ? The thrust of the first is more "horizontal," that of the second more "vertical." Let me explain. Even if Christ's resurrection bursts the normal bounds of history, there is still something unmistakably "horizontal" about it—a "before" and "after" to it. Before the resurrection he first died and then was buried. After that Christ rose again on the third day. The movement suggested by the ascension is not so much horizontal (and historical) as it is vertical. From the depths of humiliation entailed by his death on the cross, Christ has gone up into the glory of heaven.

We human beings absorb and express events in terms of time and space. The first Christians took in and stated what had happened to the person of Jesus in terms of time (the resurrection) and space (the ascension). He had risen again on the third day and ascended into heaven. Inevitably the earliest Christians reached for this language of time and space when communicating what they knew to have happened to Jesus after his crucifixion.

Admittedly Jesus' resurrection from the dead remains the central claim. Defenders of Christianity write books with such titles as *Who Moved the Stone?* I have not yet heard of any book of Christian apologetics entitled *Did He Ascend?* Nevertheless, belief in Jesus' ascension has its own special function.

One way of establishing this point could be to compare the mosaic in St. Clement's with Michelangelo's statue of the risen Christ to be found in another church of Rome, that of Santa Maria sopra Minerva. As in so many western paintings and statues of the risen Jesus, he is triumphantly alive again, but there is not much sense of his new, transformed existence. He has returned to life and, if one may put it this way, looks like a splendid athlete. But he does not come across as living now in transfigured glory.

Like Christian art, the very language of "re-surrection" itself can wrongly be taken to imply a mere "return" or "coming back" to life, as if Jesus were simply resuscitated or reanimated after his death and burial. That would be to forget how his resurrection meant his entering into an awesome new state of glory (Lk 24:26).

We need St. Clement's majestic mosaic of the gloriously transformed Christ to remind us that his resurrection was much more than a mere coming back to life under the normal conditions of our present existence. We need also the language of the feast of the Ascension. Jesus went up into heavenly glory to sit at the right hand of the Father.

That language and those images speak of Jesus sitting not near God's throne but at the Father's very right hand. He has now assumed his true place. During his earthly life

Jesus spoke to God and of God with astonishing familiarity and scandalous intimacy. He had every right to do so. He is now vindicated and shown to be truly the divine Son of God at the right hand of the eternal Father.

To be sure, the beliefs in Christ's resurrection and in his ascension converge in maintaining that even death did not finally defeat him. But these two beliefs differ or at least separately fill out the total picture for us, just as the statue in Santa Maria sopra Minerva and the mosaic in St. Clement's do. As a sign of victory over death, Michelangelo's risen Christ carries his cross. That is a useful reminder of the before and the after—of the horizontal, historical level. Jesus died and was buried and then rose victoriously from the dead. The mosaic in St. Clement's reminds us that Jesus' victory was much more than the mere reanimation of a corpse. He has entered into his final glory to be acknowledged for what he truly is, the only Son of God and divine ruler of the universe.

In brief, Easter remains the major feast of the year. But it is at our peril that we ignore the ascension and what it clarifies about Christ's true and final state.

The Acts of the Apostles pictures Christ ascending to the right hand of the Father and from there sharing in the outpouring of the Spirit (Acts 2:23). In other words, Christ's ascension into glory puts him in the position to join in sending his Spirit into the world. A later chapter attends to the risen Jesus' greatest gift to us, the Holy Spirit.

I had been going to one particular church in Rome for several years before I discovered that the ceiling contained a painting of the ascension. What had really attracted me to the church was a breathtaking painting behind the altar of the crucifixion by Guido Reni. It is a remarkable work, the only one I can think of in which Christ is still alive on the cross. Instead of the usual bowed head, Jesus is looking upward, caught in a moment of anguish and despair, almost as though he were struggling with his fate. Here is Jesus of the cry "My God, my God, why hast thou forsaken me?" of Mark's gospel, rather than the less anguished Jesus of Luke's "Father, into thy hands I commit my spirit!"

It is perhaps because this crucifixion dominates the whole church—in the evening it is lit up in such a way that it can be seen even from the square outside—that it takes so long to discover the painting of the ascension. It is only really visible from the entrance. Once you have reached the middle of the nave it is uncomfortable to crane your neck up to see it, and if you look back from the altar it is obscured by the light coming in from the upper windows. It is a weak and unconvincing work of art by any standards; set against the Reni crucifixion it is easy to miss completely. Rather like the descriptions of the ascension after the dramatic crucifixion narratives in the gospels, it is pale and fantastical. But just as now I never fail to look up at the ceiling in that church, I always arrive at the feast of the Ascension with a sense of relief after the intensity of the Easter season.

Overshadowed by the power of the crucifixion and the resurrection on one side and then by Pentecost on the other, the ascension almost seems to be an unimportant event in the life of Jesus. It takes up only a few lines in the gospel of Luke, followed by that flowery description you mention in Acts. Neither art, nor music, nor literature has treated it kindly. For some reason even the assumption of the Virgin Mary, no less fantastically an event, has caught the popular imagination more than the ascension of Christ. Who in continental Europe, for example, would think of moving the feast of the Assumption to the nearest convenient Sunday as has been the fate of the feast of the Ascension?

Yet there is something special about the feast of the Ascension. Whether it falls early or late, it comes during that magical spring month of May, unlike Easter which is celebrated during the seasonal uncertainties of March or April. Although it is years since I spent an Ascension Day in England, it still reminds me of angelic-faced choir boys singing out from church towers in the splendor of a May dawn.

In Luke's gospel we learn that the apostles went back to Jerusalem with great joy after their final parting from the Lord.

> While he blessed them, he parted from them, and was carried up into heaven. And they worshiped him, and returned to Jerusalem with great joy, and were continually in the temple blessing God.

It seems strange to us who know the whole sequence of events that there was not this same sense of peace immediately after the discovery of the resurrection. The first appearances of Christ bring, on the contrary, first fear, then anxiety, doubt, and only subsequently joy.

With the ascension all the tension has gone. The terror, remorse, betrayal, anxiety, suffering, grief, loneliness, despair, doubt, and only then the final rejoicing, which were characteristic of that first Easter and which have been relived again and again down the centuries, suddenly give way to a new calm.

What is so remarkable about the ascension is that there is nothing tragic about the final farewell to the earthly Jesus. The parting of the ascension has none of the agony and the uncertainty of the last supper.

Probably there are times in all our lives when a good-bye feels incomplete and uncertain, and we wonder how we shall face the future ahead. At other times a farewell, however sad, feels complete, as though all that should have been said has been said, all that can be done has been done, and however unsure the road may be ahead, it seems manageable. There is a sort of happiness in the sadness of these occasions.

There are also moments in our lives when it feels good to return to a normal routine. An exceptional period finally comes to an end and we have to get on with our lives. We stop being Marys sitting at the feet of the Lord and we return to being the Marthas of everyday life.

Once again most of us have probably experienced those wonderful, exhilarating moments when our normal routine is turned upside down—during a family visit, a new development at work, the arrival of someone unexpected, a new stage in our education or family life, a holiday. For a while we live passionately, hurriedly, intensely, unexpectedly, even dangerously. Then quite suddenly life returns to normal. If never quite the same again, life now has a comforting, familiar ordinariness lived in the light of the new experience. We get on with the job in hand with a new vision, a new insight, a new calm.

This for me is the place of the ascension in the church's year. After the excitement of Christmas, the toughness of Lent, the passion of Holy Week, the doubt and the joy of the resurrection, the ascension marks the end of the earthly life of Jesus but it also signals a new beginning in our old lives. The way ahead is still tough, but never as tough as what has gone before. In the early May dawn there is a calm and certainty which the turbulent March or April Easter season does not provide. At Easter we are still struggling to throw off the end of winter; with the feast of the Ascension we are finally through to the spring.

13

"He Will Come Again To Judge the Living and the Dead"

Many people used to take their picture of Christ's second coming from Michelangelo's huge fresco in the Sistine Chapel here in Rome. That full-scale treatment of the general judgment shows a powerful, terrifying Christ dominating the world while the dead rise to be rewarded or punished according to their deeds.

Michelangelo includes in that scene of final judgment the righteous, whose merits will bring them through to glory. But it is the slippery ease of sin and the horrors of hell that the somber masterpiece more readily evokes. It lets the old dread of a punishing God continue in a new form—as the punishing Christ.

In my youth I heard warnings proclaimed from pulpits about that terrible scrutiny from Christ which we will face at the end. I drew my main consolation from the hope that when he came again, it would be during my lifetime. As one of those living then, I would have to join the line for judgment but at least I would escape the pain of death. Otherwise the second coming seemed a thoroughly frightening prospect that preyed on my scrupulous conscience.

More than fifty years ago one of my fellow Australians persuaded hundreds of people to pay for seats in an outdoor theater to be constructed on a headland facing the entrance of Sydney's harbor. The ticket-holders would have a privileged view of Christ when he staged his return and came on low clouds between the cliffs that open into that majestic harbor.

But Christ has been slow in coming again. Even for many believers his second coming has lost much of its power to instill awe and mobilize action. The last judgment can seem of little interest to any but art historians and sectarian fundamentalists.

A pity! The final coming of Christ gives a great sense of urgency to much of the New Testament. Our Bible ends with the prayer, "Come, Lord Jesus" (Rev 22:20). Things can go wrong when we fail to be touched by those words, "Yes, I am coming soon, bringing my recompense, to repay everyone for what he has done. I am the Alpha and the Omega, the first and the last, the beginning and the end" (Rev 22:12–13).

A number of important truths are suggested by the last article in the Creed to address itself to Christ. First, he will appear before the whole human race and not just over the waters of Sydney's harbor. At his first coming Jesus drew large crowds but he limited his brief ministry to a corner of the Mediterranean world. As risen from the dead, he is now actively present not only through the eucharist and in the sacraments but in many other ways. In Our Lady of the Dunes, a church on the coast of Belgium, the tabernacle is covered with images of human faces, male and female, young and old, serene and suffering. The tabernacle brilliantly conveys the sense that we can find Christ in all our brothers and sisters. Jesus' words about the last judgment (Mt 25:31–46) show how he identifies himself with all those who in their various needs have a claim on our practical love. He comes to us now behind the faces of the five thousand million human beings living on our planet. They are all signs and sacraments of his presence now. But it is a veiled presence. We do not see, hear and touch Christ directly and immediately. At his second coming he will confront all people: those who have never even heard his name, those who have known and followed him, those who have known him but taken him for granted or drifted away, those who have heard his name but found his followers hard to accept. All will know Christ when he comes at the end openly and in glory.

Christ is truth and goodness personified. His second coming will unmask the greedy dishonesty and selfish malice that so often pass themselves off as true values by which to live. For all their faults, human beings naturally hunger for the answers to those two fundamental questions: What is the real meaning of things? What is ultimately good for us? At the end, truth will out and goodness will be known. We will emerge from the shadows and half-light of our caves to face things as they really are.

Our human solidarity is a third item indicated by Christ's final coming. We will all belong together, both those living at the end and those millions resurrected from the dead to face our judge and savior. The day of individualism, tribalism and nationalism will be finally over. As members of the one human race, all men and women will be confronted with Christ, the omega-point of us all. The old political religious and social barriers will disappear. To adapt St. Paul's language, "there will be neither Jew nor Greek, there will be neither slave nor free, there will be neither male nor female; we will all be one before Christ Jesus" (Gal 3:28). For good or evil, we form one human family. That basic reality will be reasserted at the end.

In St. Matthew's vivid scene of the last judgment everyone will be gathered before the glorious throne of the Son of Man and divided into the sheep and the goats. After judgment the goats on the left side will be dispatched into eternal punishment, the sheep on the right into eternal life (Mt 25:31–46). As much or more than any other section of the New Testament, this scene from Matthew has shaped Christian thinking about what will happen to us at the end: some to suffer the irrevocable fate of hell and others to enjoy the endless happiness of heaven. Judgment will turn

123

on whether or not we have visited the sick, fed the hungry, welcomed strangers and in other ways shown a practical love toward those with basic human needs that cry out for our help.

This fourth truth about Christ's final coming highlights the radical and lasting importance of our human liberty. We can easily drop into the habit of playing down the enduring significance of our free actions. Things can be changed; we can take back our decisions; sinful failures may be dismissed as mere temporary blemishes on our record. The scene from Matthew gives the lie to all that. For good or evil, our free decisions have eternal consequences.

At the same time, can we conclude from Matthew and similar New Testament texts that some, perhaps very many human beings will finish up forever in hell? At the end of a life given to praying, thinking and writing, Hans Urs von Balthasar concluded that we have no right to claim categorically that some men and women will suffer for all eternity in hell. This fate however remains a clear possibility: freedom means that we could radically and definitively reject God and our fellow human beings. A deliberately adopted posture of hatred could take us that far. On our side we have no guarantee that we could never be so freely malicious as to condemn ourselves to hell.

But the Christ who will come as judge is the same Jesus who first came to seek and to save those who were lost.

A close relative of mine, who has spent her life caring for strangers and in a thousand ways showing real love to those in need, still wants to have sung at her funeral that beautiful hymn to the Lord's mercy, "Amazing Grace." Her instinct is profoundly right. What will ultimately matter at the end will not be our good deeds or bad deeds, but the love of God shining through the compassionate face of Christ. His mercy, rather than our freedom, will have the final word.

This fifth truth about the second coming was put to me over a pizza recently. I had walked down the Via del Corso to find Sergio, the only urban hermit I know in Rome. He lives in a tiny apartment just off the Piazza del Popolo, and after a day of prayer and reading emerges around seven each evening to eat his one daily meal near the oven in a tiny *trattoria*. That day he had been reading and praying over Psalm 50, "Have mercy on me, God, in your kindness." Sergio sliced through the cheese, shook his gray hair and assured me: "God does not punish. God accepts all and saves all." Outside the evening traffic roared by. But Sergio had taken me back to Paul and what the apostle wrote about the mercy of God that through Christ brings salvation to the whole world (Rom 11:32).

What Sergio said and Paul wrote justifies seeing the second coming as the third stage of God's good news for us. That is the feeling evoked and encouraged by the second eucharistic acclamation: "Dying you destroyed our death, rising you restored our life. Lord Jesus, come in glory." His second coming will crown and complete the freedom and life already given us through his death and resurrection.

Jesus will come again to judge the living and the dead. But so far from being a terrifying threat as Michelangelo might lead us to think, that belief should make us pray with joyful hope, "Come, Lord Jesus."

I suppose that everyone finds certain parts of the Creed difficult, just as parts of the Bible seem more difficult to digest than others. For some it may be the virginal conception, for others the empty tomb. For me it is the last judgment.

There was a time when the last judgment didn't bother me much. I thought that it seemed reasonable enough to divide the good from the bad at the day of reckoning. In any case I, certainly very much less humble than you, was going to make sure that I was among the sheep on that last day even though, secretly, I rather preferred goats as animals to sheep.

Those were the days when the parable of the prodigal son seemed totally incomprehensible to me. How was it possible, I reasoned, that the fellow who had always tried hard was put in the shade by his good-for-nothing brother? What justice was this? What was the point of trying to be good and helpful if the other fellow got all the attention from his father?

I suppose it was when I began to understand the joy of the father at the return of his lost son that I started to have difficulties with the idea of a last judgment. Gradually I also became aware of the fact that every time I went back to the Vatican Museum I liked the Sistine Chapel less and less. That massive wall of Michelangelo's last judgment seemed ever more like a picture out of those terrifying books of cautionary tales—luckily now out of fashion— with those painful illustrations of what would happen to children who played with matches or chewed their nails or didn't eat their food.

I preferred instead to wander slowly through the other magnificent parts of the museum which are so often overlooked in the headlong dash to the Sistine Chapel. Why miss the more gentle, reflective Raphael Loggia, or the map room where you can discover how our knowledge of the earth has grown and changed, or the marvel of the detailed needlework in those intricate tapestries sewn by unknown hands in close communion one with another? Why not gaze out at the peaceful gardens from the open windows rather than join the mad rush with thousands of others down those dark, tortuous stairs to gaze for a few hurried moments at Michelangelo's disdainful-looking, al-most menacing Christ banishing the bad from the good? There is no doubt for me that, like your friend Sergio, I would prefer to contemplate the saving, redeeming face of Jesus.

Even the words "last" and "judgment" seem difficult to reconcile with the love the father has for his lost son. "Last" is so final a concept. It doesn't allow for the possibility of another chance, of just one more try; "judgment" seems no less harsh a term. Whether we come from a culture which holds them in reverence or ill-repute, judges are remote, even forbidding beings. They administer laws, deal with crimes and mete out punishments. Theirs is not a world of sins and forgiveness, or at least only incidentally so.

Perhaps my dislike of the whole idea of a last judgment is further increased by the fact that those who spend their time looking for the signs of a second coming are a bizarre, usually unreliable lot, rather like your Sydney hoaxer.

Nearly two thousand years after the first coming of Jesus it might seem vain to speculate on the times and places of his second coming. But does the manner of Christ's first appearance on earth give us any clues as to the manner of his return?

It is perhaps worth remembering that for centuries the Jewish people expected the arrival of a savior, just as we wait for the return of that savior. But the messiah who finally came was not the messiah they were expecting. Bound by old ideas, traditions and concepts, many of the Jews to whom Jesus came were not able to accept him. Is there perhaps a danger that at the moment of the second coming we too shall shut ourselves in our churches and reject the final call? Are we as Christians, like the Jews before us, still blind to many of the mysteries of our faith? Or shall we be ready, like those courageous early Christians who left the safety of their traditions and synagogues, to set off on the road to who knows where?

The whole concept of the second coming is something of a mystery. But if we look on it as the fulfillment of the first coming rather than a final judgment, we are faced with an exciting challenge rather than a dire warning.

A second coming implies that the first coming is part but not all of our Christian history. The ascension, followed by Pentecost, seems to form a perfect ending to the Christian story. Jesus returns to the Father and sends the Holy Spirit to guide and comfort us. But this is not the end. We are to expect more. Jesus is to come again, we say in the Creed. We are not therefore just observers of past events, trying to live as Christ would have us live while remembering historical highlights of his birth, life, death, resurrection and ascension. Instead we are active participants in a continuing Christian story which looks toward a promised future. Therefore what we do now, today, really matters. Just as the choices of Adam and Eve, Mary and Joseph were of vital importance for the relationship of God and man, so our choices, in a lesser way, have a place in the course of Christian history.

We are in a very real way the product of our own choices and those of others. At birth we have an infinity of possibilities ahead of us. As our lives continue, those possibilities narrow down. We make one decision rather than another. That moment of taking this turning instead of that passes and we are out on another road. We may have made the wrong choice and we can turn back, but the lost son who turns for home still takes the years of his aimless wanderings with him. While there may be a new life ahead of him, he is still very much a product of the old. At any stage of our Christian journey we may choose another fork in the road or retrace our steps, but what we have seen and done on the way stays with us forever. And when we come to the end of the road, all our decisions, in this direction or that, will add up to a final whole, good or bad. In other words our choices are not idle whims of little count but, as you say, decisions which have eternal consequences.

The loss of the sense of urgency about the second coming which you mention has perhaps tended to dull our understanding of the importance of the present. How many of us live as though today really were our last? As though we were only minutes away from having to render an account of our actions? That second coming doesn't seem real any longer and certainly isn't of overwhelming significance in most of our lives. Can we even be sure that we shall be ready for the second coming when it happens? May we not find that like the foolish maidens in the parable we have used up all the oil in our lamps before the bridegroom arrives? For all our preparation shall we, like the Jews before us, fail to recognize the savior when he comes again? How shall we as Christians know the messiah when he returns?

Perhaps some of the answers can be found in the subject of the next chapter, the Holy Spirit. It was, after all, thanks to the power of the Holy Spirit, as we read in the gospel of Luke, that the devout, aging Simeon recognized the baby Jesus in the temple at Jerusalem. Simeon did not have the knowledge of Mary, the love of Joseph for his wife, the scientific expertise of the wise men or the living Christ who guided the apostles. No signs, no miracles, no living example: just a baby and his parents. But Simeon knew that the Savior had come.

"And inspired by the Holy Spirit he came to the temple; and when the parents brought in the child Jesus to do for him according to the custom of the law, he took him in his arms and blessed God and said: 'Lord, now lettest thou thy servant depart in peace, according to thy word; for mine eyes have seen thy salvation which thou hast prepared in the presence of all peoples, a light for a revelation to the Gentiles and for glory to thy people Israel' " (Lk 2:27–32).

How many of us will be blessed with the insight of Simeon when the final day comes?

14

"I Believe in the Holy Spirit"

"The Holy Ghost is in the fields." For years those words from an Irish country writer haunted me. Like him I had grown up on a farm and marveled at the mystery of new life: the fluffy chickens darting ahead of the hens, the white rings of flowers on the pear trees, wild rabbits enjoying the grass on an early summer's evening. But before reading Patrick Kavanagh, I had never thought of all that simple life and growth as the work of God's Spirit.

Yet right from the book of Genesis our scriptures witness to God's Spirit that brings life and growth. It comes then as no surprise in John's gospel when the risen Jesus breathes on his disciples and says, "Receive the Holy Spirit." The life-giving breath or Spirit of God will animate the community of disciples as the church begins to live, grow and move out.

Whether in the fields, the church or human society, the Holy Spirit is at work, bringing life and growth. That may happen, as in the story of the first Pentecost (Acts 2:1–4), with fiery flames, talk in tongues and the sound of a strong, driving wind. Or growth may come as silently as blades of grass springing from the soil or white blossoms opening along the branches of fruit trees.

In the story of Jesus' life and growth, the Holy Spirit is there from the beginning to the end. It is through the power of the Holy Spirit that Jesus is conceived and comes into our midst. Full of the Spirit, Jesus comes away from his baptism in the River Jordan to be led by the Spirit into the desert for forty days of prayer and fasting. He returns "in the power of the Spirit" (Lk 4:14) and begins his ministry as one "anointed" by "the Spirit of the Lord" to announce "the good news to the poor" and let "broken victims go free" (Lk 4:16–21). At the end, when Jesus dies and a soldier stabs his side with a spear, blood and water flow out, symbolizing the living waters of the Spirit gushing into the world (Jn 7:37–39; 19:34). Then through God's Spirit (Rom 8:11) Jesus is raised to become a spiritual body (1 Cor 15:42–50) and "a life-giving spirit" (1 Cor 15:45).

We will never properly grasp the whole story of Jesus unless we recall the role of the Holy Spirit in bringing about Jesus' being *with* us, *for* us, and *in* us. Through the incarnation Jesus becomes present with us. In his life and ministry he gave himself for us. As risen from the dead, Jesus began a new communion of life that St. John presents as a mutual indwelling, we in Christ and Christ in us (Jn 15:4–5; 17:21–23). It is the Holy Spirit who empowers the Christ story, from the incarnation to the resurrection, so that Christ is not only with us but also for us and even in us.

In the Creed the Holy Spirit comes as the third divine person who is the "object" of the profession "I/we believe in." First, we express faith in God, the Father almighty, who is named in a special way as "creator" of the universe. Then we profess our faith in Jesus Christ, who saved us through his life, death and resurrection. Third, we express faith in the Holy Spirit who brings the forgiveness of sins and gives life to the church.

As sanctifier, the Holy Spirit forms the culmination of the movement from the Father-creator through the Son-savior. At the same time, the Spirit initiates a movement of return—back to the final coming of the Son and the full revelation of the Father in the new creation at the end of time.

The tripartite structure of the Creed unpacks and develops those trinitarian formulas which we find at key points in the New Testament. Matthew's gospel ends with the risen Jesus sending his followers to make disciples of all nations and baptize them in the name of the Father and of the Son and of the Holy Spirit (Mt 28:19). Paul rounds off his second letter to the Corinthians with a blessing that has become an alternate greeting at the beginning of mass: "The grace of the Lord Jesus Christ and the love of God and the fellowship of the Holy Spirit be with you all" (2 Cor 13:14).

These two trinitarian formulas reflect the faith and experience of early believers. With the Father and the Son, the Holy Spirit is at work in the sacrament that turns human beings into Christians: baptism. The Holy Spirit belongs also to the best blessings and greetings that we Christians can exchange with one another.

Before, however, there was any question of Christians baptizing new members of the church or blessing established believers, the Holy Spirit was imparted to the world in and through Christ's dying and rising. Often artists have appreciated better than theologians how the first Good Friday and Easter Sunday fully and finally revealed the tripersonal God for us. Here I am thinking especially of the "mercy-seat" paintings and carvings of the crucifixion. The Father receives the cross which bears the dead body of the Son, or else simply holds the corpse in his arms. At times the posture and luminosity of Jesus' body point to the resurrection which is soon to take place. Above or below, the Holy Spirit appears under the form of a dove. The "mercy-seat" compositions maintain a thoroughly trinitarian vision of Calvary—with the Holy Spirit present alongside the Father and the Son.

In his famous icon Rublev (ca. 1360–1430) also associates the Trinity with Christ's dying and rising. He does this through the eucharist, the sacrificial meal in which we proclaim the death and resurrection of the Lord until he comes again in glory. The icon (now kept in a Moscow gallery) represents the Father, Son and Holy Spirit as three figures seated around a table. A chalice on the table clearly links the Trinity with the eucharist and the story of Christ's passion and death.

My last two paragraphs have spoken of the Holy Spirit being revealed in and through Christ's dying and rising from the dead. What has to be added, however, is the centuries-long process Christians needed to undergo before they quite clearly recognized the personal identity of the Holy Spirit. The challenge took a double form. Christ was/is obviously a distinct person. But was/is he truly and fully divine? As the Spirit of God, the Holy Spirit is obviously divine. But is the Spirit a distinct person?

The first general council of the church, which met at Nicea (now Iznik in modern Turkey) in 325, clearly taught the divine identity of Christ. The next general council of the church (at Constantinople in 381) officially acknowledged the personal identity of the Holy Spirit as the third person of the divine Trinity. Those two councils were not inventing new teachings but rather finally making fully explicit what believers had experienced and held about Christ and the Spirit from the beginning.

Our Creed, therefore, rightly professes belief *in* the Holy Spirit as the third divine person alongside the Father and the Son. At the same time, right from the origins of Christianity the faithful have recognized that they believe not only in the Holy Spirit but *because of* the Holy Spirit. The divine Spirit makes things possible and makes things happen: personal faith, the forgiveness of sins, the life of the sacraments, the whole church's basic fidelity to the original message of and about Christ, fresh insights into and new applications of that message, and loving communication between individuals and groups where all communication seemed to have broken down. Everywhere God's Spirit is at work, humanizing and divinizing people within and beyond Christianity.

In the sacrament of penance the prayer of absolution acknowledges the Holy Spirit sent "among us for the forgiveness of sins." After recognizing how "all life" and "all holiness" comes by the working of the Holy Spirit, the third eucharistic prayer invokes God's Spirit:

> And so Father, we bring you these gifts
> We ask you to make them holy by the power of your Spirit,
> that they may become the body and blood
> of your Son, our Lord Jesus Christ,
> at whose command we celebrate this eucharist.

These two prayers, taken from the sacrament of reconciliation and the mass, typify the way Roman Catholics and other Christians acknowledge God's Spirit to be at work bringing life, holiness and growth to a wounded human race.

Centuries ago Australia had the name "The Land of the Holy Spirit." Not only Australia but also the entire planet could well be called "The World of the Holy Spirit."

Such a vision of the Holy Spirit's activity that takes us far beyond Paddy Kavanagh's little farm in Ireland can seem exaggerated and incredible to those who believe in God but do not share Christian faith. But even more mysterious and difficult is the belief that precedes any talk about the Spirit's activity. Before speaking of a church made holy and catholic through the Spirit, the communion of saints effected by the Spirit and the rest, the Creed professes belief in the Holy Spirit, as well as belief in the Father and the Son.

The mystery of the Holy Spirit's activity is really nothing in comparison with the utterly basic mystery of the Trinity: one God but three persons. Artists have wrestled with the mystery. The "mercy seat" representations use one cross to link Father, Son and Holy Spirit. Rublev links his three figures by the one table and the one chalice, but above all by the divine harmony and unity that pervade the whole composition.

Personally my own faith in our tripersonal God finds its support and nourishment in very simple things. I hear John Henry Newman's lines, set to music by Edward Elgar: "Firmly I believe and truly/God is three, and God is one." Or else I recall St. Patrick's classic illustration of the divine mystery: the shamrock leaf which is one but also three.

Finally, there is something millions of Christians do a number of times every day. They make the sign of the cross "in the name of the Father, and of the Son and of the Holy Spirit." That extremely simple profession of faith in the Trinity points to the great truth at the start of Christian history: it was through the dying and rising of Christ that the Trinity was finally revealed and the power of the Holy Spirit sent into our world.

The power of the Holy Spirit is something like the power of love; those who have experienced it know what it is but have difficulty describing it to the satisfaction of others. "You just know," was the answer my mother once gave to the childhood inquiry about how you knew if you loved someone. At the time I considered the reply disappointing and unsatisfactory. I wanted easy solutions and precise guidelines. But how right and how wise she was to give me none!

Attempts to define the Holy Spirit are no less difficult. Neither God the Father nor God the Son presents quite the same problems as God the Holy Spirit. The terms "Holy Spirit" and the old fashioned "Holy Ghost" are a measure themselves of the difficulties. Spirits or ghosts are elusive things, with no material existence, deeply experienced by the few and discredited by the many.

Western definitions of the Holy Spirit cling to abstract terms and images. We have the dove, the wind, the fire and the sudden light. We use symbols which range from gentleness to overwhelming power, from quiet to deafening noise, from unity to separation. We struggle with the complications of the Trinity and refuse to have the simple understanding of children. Of all the difficult questions I have had to answer from children about the relationship of God and man I have never had one on the Trinity.

Is the idea of three distinct beings in one holy unity really so outlandish? The concept of separately functioning parts which make up a single united whole is one we meet almost daily. In our own lives we experience the distinct roles of daughter-wife-mother or son-husband-father integrated into one person with each separate function adding to the whole. How little, for instance, the daughter understands the mother until she in turn has children of her own. Is it really so problematic to make that extra leap of the imagination to take in the holy one in three?

Perhaps some of the difficulties arise because we tend to separate the Father, Son and Holy Spirit in time and place. In the Creed we state our belief in chronological sequence. Equally in the church's year the feast of Pentecost comes after those devoted to the Son. We are therefore inclined to see the Holy Spirit as the last of the three, almost as a second-best alternative sent by Jesus after his work was done.

Even if we take only the miraculous transformation in the apostles at Pentecost, we are forced to acknowledge that the Holy Spirit was not just a comforter or substitute for the risen Christ. It was the Holy Spirit who inspired those ordinary Galileans, forced them out of their rooms in Jerusalem where they had huddled since the crucifixion, and sent them fearlessly back and forth across the then-known world.

Rather than being the first great manifestation of the power of the Holy Spirit, Pentecost is the culmination of what has gone before. We acknowledge the power of the Holy Spirit at the conception of Christ. In Peter's long speech at Pentecost—so out of character with the apostle we have known until then—we read of Joel's Old Testament prophecy of the power of the Holy Spirit. If we go even further back to the first verse of the Bible, we find:

> In the beginning God created the heavens and the earth. The earth was without form and void, and darkness was upon the face of the deep; and the spirit of God was moving over the face of the waters.

Even before the first act of creation we have the spirit of God in motion. Whether or not we take this reference to the spirit, usually footnoted as the wind, as the first reference to the Holy Spirit, we have here those two vital elements—air and water—which even the early writers of Genesis understood as the beginnings of all life. We come full circle if we then return to the Creed, this time to the fuller Nicene Creed where we state: "I believe in the Holy Spirit, the Lord, the giver of life."

I must admit that I probably would not have explored the Old Testament references to the Holy Spirit had not your mention of the Rublev icon sent me wandering in new directions. I knew other works by the famous Russian monk and icon painter but not this one. Having tracked down a reproduction I found to my surprise that it was called the Old Testament Trinity. So firmly was the Holy Spirit associated with Pentecost in my mind that I had not thought of the third person of the Trinity in terms of the Old Testament. I was therefore fascinated to discover that some of the earliest paintings of the Trinity, found in the Christian catacombs, were in fact of Abraham, Sarah and the three wayfaring angels of the Old Testament story (Gen 18:1–8), with the three angels representing the Trinity.

Here in the Rublev icon we have the link between the

old and the new. Abraham has gone, except for his house in the background, although the meal described in the Old Testament remains. But, as you point out, the meal in the Rublev icon is clearly symbolic of Christ's new sacrifice, relived in the eucharist.

What also delighted me about the Rublev icon was the similarity of the three angels. So alike are their faces that it is difficult to tell them apart. Here for the first time I saw the Holy Spirit not marked off from the Father and the Son in the usual imagery of a dove, but together with the Father and the Son in the person of an angel. But more than anything else Rublev's icon illustrated for me that interweaving of the east and west of Christianity. Here in the Russian icon was not only the common root but also the separate branches of our faith: the separate figures of the Father, Son and Holy Spirit united in those look-alike faces of the three angels, symbols of our commonly shared Trinity.

15

"The Holy, Catholic Church"

Years ago a young friend of mine told me how he had gone to an important tennis tournament and started chatting with a girl sitting next to him. The subject of religion came up and, rather directly, he asked her, "What are you?" "I'm a Catholic, worse luck!" she replied with a frown.

That was the period of the late 1960s and early 1970s when many Roman Catholics and other Christians took the position, "Jesus, yes. Church, no." At the beginning of the 1990s anti-institutional feelings have waned somewhat. For many people however, it is still not easy to identify with the church.

Nevertheless, in the story of Israel and then in Christianity itself God invites men and women to receive salvation through a community. As Martin Luther remarked, "those who want to find Christ must first find the church." We know about Jesus through the church (Rom 10:14–17). We become his disciples by being baptized into the church (Rom 6:1–11) and remain as such by celebrating the eucharist together until he comes again (1 Cor 11:23–26). The Christian religion is essentially social, never a matter of just God, Jesus and myself.

During his earthly life Jesus had been *the* visible sign and living symbol of his Father. This is a truth classically expressed by Jesus' words to Philip, "He who has seen me has seen the Father" (Jn 14:9). With his death, resurrection and the end of the Easter appearances (1 Cor 15:8), the risen Lord remains present (Mt 28:20) but is no longer directly seen and heard. We do not literally and immediately hear his voice or see his face. We cannot reach out and touch him as people sometimes did during his lifetime.

What we see and hear and touch is his church, the community which had been prepared for over the centuries and which fully came into being at the first Pentecost. That community is the visible, living sign of the risen Lord's presence and of his desire to bring home to the Father all men and women of all times and places. The New Testament thinks of the church as, above all, a community of love that is Christ's beautiful bride.

One Saturday morning in Rome succeeded in finally communicating to me this truth about the church. That day I was blessed by the chance of celebrating a wedding in St. Peter's basilica. The bride was Japanese, the bridegroom Australian. After the wedding ceremony and the mass, we walked out of the huge church into the square to have some photographs taken on the steps, under the obelisk and by the fountains. The sun came out, warming thousands of visitors who were gazing at the majesty of St. Peter's, ambling across the cobblestones or moving slowly back to their buses. The newly married couple, especially the bride, changed all that in a moment.

For an hour the radiantly beautiful girl in her long, classical wedding dress became the center of St. Peter's Square. That Saturday morning she put a smile on thousands of faces. A crowd of Italian teenagers ran up to wish her long life and happiness. A line of Korean tourists greeted her with enthusiasm. Europeans, Africans and Americans swept toward her with their congratulations. The whole world seemed to be there rejoicing in the marriage.

What drew that reaction from those thousands of people? The special beauty of the bride in her exquisite gown obviously touched their hearts. Then the sight of two young people committing themselves to each other for a lifetime always proves a powerful sign of hope in a world where the future can look precarious and lasting fidelity in short supply. In this case everyone could see that it was an interracial marriage, between a Japanese and someone of European origin. The decision of the couple to pledge themselves across cultural and national divisions signaled a courageous love that was willing to deal with any difficulty and pay any price. Finally, the unexpected grace of it all must have spoken to many pilgrims and tourists. Who had promised them that they would meet and greet a lovely bride that sunny morning in St. Peter's Square?

Thinking later about the whole experience, I found it throwing fresh light on the New Testament's language about all of us in the church. This new community is the "glorious" bride of the risen Lord (Eph 5:21–33), and is moving toward the future Jerusalem which is to "come down out of heaven made ready like a bride adorned for her husband" (Rev 21:2, 9).

Here and now the church is called to attract the whole world by her bridal beauty. What is lovely and radiant evokes joy in others. The church's radiant devotion should do just that: draw together the peoples of the earth and put smiles on their faces.

St. Paul knew that Christ had put an end to the old barriers that had separated people for so long: "There is no such thing as Jew and Greek, slave and freeman, male and female; for you are all one person in Christ Jesus" (Gal 3:28). Those who rejoiced at the young couple in St. Peter's Square could have said something like that: "In Christ there is no such thing as Japanese or Australian, for they are made one through their courageous love." The marriage of my two friends symbolized the new unity of the Christian community which overcomes old divisions through the fresh life of the resurrection.

From the time of the New Testament, the church has

been pictured as Christ's bride. But such images can become routine phrases that lose their power. The unexpected grace of a lovely Japanese girl in St. Peter's Square put life back into that image for me. She symbolized what the whole church is and is invited to be: a radiant bride who joyfully draws all nations to her risen Lord.

We need time to think about the nature and destiny of the community founded by Christ and guided by his Holy Spirit. In fact, the Apostles' Creed offers us the chance of two chapters—this one looking more at the nature of the church and the next at her destiny.

"Holy" and "catholic" shape the vision of the church in this chapter. Holiness belongs primarily to God, who through majestic sacredness is set infinitely apart from sinful human beings. In Isaiah's vision the seraphim cry out "holy" three times, thus emphasizing the fullness of holiness which belongs to God alone (Is 6:1–5). His profound religious experience in the temple at Jerusalem inspires awe and even terror in the prophet. Face to face with God, he feels lost, unclean and deeply sinful (Is 6:5–7).

During the eucharist the Sanctus acclaims the awesome nature of God by echoing the seraphims' cry of "holy, holy, holy." All the same, believers know that through being baptized and incorporated into Christ, they no longer stand "outside" but have come to share in the very holiness of God. As St. Paul reminds the community at Corinth, they now form a consecrated temple in which the Holy Spirit dwells (1 Cor 3:16–17). The apostle is well aware of the many sinful faults that disfigure the Corinthian community. Chapter after chapter of his first letter to them lists their failures. There are quarrels that have divided them into parties. The cases of sexual immorality even include an incestuous relationship. Christians have been bringing law suits against each other. Some are eating well, getting drunk and neglecting to feed the poorer members of the community. Despite these and other sin-

142

ful failures, Paul knows, however, that baptism has indelibly consecrated the Corinthian Christians (1 Cor 6:11) and called them all to a life of holiness (1 Cor 1:2).

The letter to the Ephesians pictures the whole church as the beautiful bride of Christ. Yet that same letter acknowledges that Christians at Ephesus must still give up sinful, pagan ways of acting (Eph 4:17–5:20). The bridal beauty and holiness of the church have not yet reached their perfection.

The letter to the Galatians proudly proclaims the new, united community Christ has created. He has put an end to the old religious, social and cultural barriers that have divided people (Gal 3:28). Nevertheless, that very same letter witnesses to the way a wrong-headed legalism was disturbing and dividing the Christian churches in Galatia.

In our own century the bishops at the Second Vatican Council (1962–1965) repeated what was essentially the same message about the church that we hear from St. Paul's letters. Through faith and baptism all Christians are organically linked with Christ and born again to become a holy people (1 Pet 1:3; 2:9–10). Our common call to holiness involves, however, a continual struggle with the forces of evil (Eph 6:10–20) which threaten to harm and desecrate what we all are—the temple of the Holy Spirit. As Vatican II recognized, the church *is* essentially a holy and consecrated community. But she is *also* a community in constant need of reform and renewal.

The holiness of the church comes from someone whose influence shows up publicly (Gal 5:22–23) but who is not yet directly seen—the Holy Spirit sent by Christ and his Father. To call the church "catholic," however, points to something out there in the open, the visible body of Christians found in practically every country on the face of the earth. The commission "to make disciples of all nations" (Mt 28:18–20) has brought about a worldwide community. Even if they are still only a minority of the human race, the followers of Jesus Christ truly make the church "catholic." They are visibly there across the world.

I have lost touch with my young friend of the late 1960s and never knew the girl he met at the tennis tournament. But I pray for her. Perhaps during the 1970s or 1980s she came to appreciate the extraordinary blessing involved in being baptized into "the holy, catholic church." It meant her consecration to a life of radiant holiness that would help reveal the risen Lord to all the peoples of the earth. If she realizes that, she would say today with a smile, "I'm a Catholic Christian, thank God."

In one of the early chapters of Thomas Mann's novel *Dr. Faustus* the protagonist Adrian Leverkühn makes the following remarks during a discussion with his fellow theological students:

> I know of course that it is the most talented among you, those who have read Kierkegaard, who place truth, even ethical truth, entirely in the subjective, and reject with horror everything that savors of herd existence. But I cannot go with you in your radicalism —which certainly will not long persist, as it is student licence—I cannot go with you in your separation, after Kierkegaard, of Church and Christianity. I see the Church, even as she is today, secularized and reduced to the bourgeois, a citadel of order, an institution for objective disciplining, canalizing, banking-up of the religious life, which without her would fall victim of subjectivist demoralization, to a chaos of divine and demonic powers, to a world of fantastic uncanniness, an ocean of daemony. To separate Church and religion means to give up separating the religious from madness.

It is in fact as Leverkühn gives up studying to become a Lutheran pastor, a calling which he decides is too undemanding for his intellectual capacities, that his difficulties begin. Turning away from what he considers to be the dullness of his theological studies and choosing instead the demands of musical composition, he makes his pact with the devil, so guaranteeing both his greatest triumph but also his own madness and death.

The theory that great art is somehow connected with madness and decadence recurs often in late nineteenth and early twentieth century literature. The idea that the church is a bastion against disorder and chaos in society is also a commonly held point of view. But in this passage Leverkühn implicitly raises yet another point: Can Christians be Christians without the church?

Individuals can and do live on their own, outside the conventional confines of a given community. Children can and do survive and grow up without their parents. For all sorts of reasons children may find themselves on their own. Their parents may have separated. Violence may break out in the family. Economic hardship may set in. Children may feel alienated, may not accept the same standards of behavior as their parents, may break away from the family or may be removed to safer or more adequate surroundings. The child survives and lives on, but something is missing. By force of circumstances—intellectual, social, political, economic—the child has been deprived of the right kind of family life.

Families of course are not necessarily those ideal, loving, giving, understanding units we should like them to be. They may be downright aggressive, repressive and damaging to the well-being of the child. But few would disagree that at its best there is little to compare with family life for the welfare of children.

You emphasize, Gerald, the imagery of the bride in your descriptions of the church. The bride is certainly glorious and triumphant but her moment is only the beginning of the long family history. It is only the start of the growth and development of a relationship first between the husband and wife and then between the parents and their children.

We pay homage to the bride. But isn't it the wife and then the mother whom we really love? The bride's moment is fleeting, but that of the wife and mother ends only in death. The bride is beautiful, magnificent, perhaps even self-centered; the mother is patient, understanding, forgiving, long-suffering, perhaps severe, maybe sometimes mistaken, but always loving.

Have you ever noticed how quickly wedding photos look dated or how often children laugh to think that their parents once looked like that? Wedding photos soon end up faded in the family album just as the glorious wedding dress is packed carefully away in an old trunk. The bride has gone but the wife and mother lives on; young, middle-aged, old, sad or happy, smart or shabby, healthy or sick, she is always there.

If you are to stop at the photo of the bride it is like seeing only part of the story. It would be like giving up after Christ's triumphal entry into Jerusalem. You would never witness the passion, the crucifixion and the resurrection. All are moments the bride will encounter when the bells have stopped ringing, the toasts are over and the last guest has said goodbye. It was after all Adrian Leverkühn's mother who gathered up the broken musician—mad, violent, half paralyzed—at the close of Thomas Mann's massive novel, to take him home and minister to him until the end of his days.

16

"The Communion of Saints"

For a concise dictionary of theology that a friend is writing with me, we have defined the communion of saints as follows: "The spiritual union between Christ and all Christians, whether already in heaven (or purgatory) or still living here on earth." Compared with the way I experience the communion of saints, such a definition inevitably seems bloodless. The experience itself reaches deep into my memories and hopes.

As I think back to the events of my childhood and boyhood, memory fetches up the faces of many relatives and friends who are long dead but who remain living presences in the Lord. I sense the way they accompany my life, and I look forward immensely to being with them forever when my own pilgrimage is over.

One of them was an Irishman, Fr. William Hackett, who in the 1940s lived in semi-retirement at the boarding-school that I attended in Melbourne (Australia). We boys all believed that this slightly stooped priest, with a brush of white hair over his twinkling eyes, had to leave his native Ireland in the early 1920s because of his connections with rebel leaders. This gentlemanly old priest gathered many of us for political and cultural discussions, encouraged wide reading through a special collection of books he made available to us, and effected what in later jargon was called a "raising of consciousness." He wanted to lead us young boys through study, discussion and prayer to share his ideal of becoming a gentleman, a scholar and a saint. He lived by those words he loved to quote from Léon Bloy: "The only sadness is not to love God, not to be a saint."

In the 1950s Fr. Hackett met with a fatal accident one bleak evening when he went out to give Benediction of the Blessed Sacrament at a nearby convent. He declined the offer of a younger priest to take his place. Under his umbrella in the drizzling rain he failed to see a car coming. He lay on the road too broken to be moved until the ambulance arrived. In the hospital Fr. Hackett lingered on and gradually recovered consciousness. "I've had a bit of an upset," he observed. After a week or two death came to this wonderful priest, who used to say with perfect sincerity: "The love of God is the greatest adventure in life."

The communion of saints embraces those who have already passed from this life to our final home with God. Their memorial cards fill my breviary or book of daily prayer: Agnes with a warm smile playing across her face; Jock whom I hoped to welcome in Rome but who died suddenly at the age of fifty-four; Olis who lived on the same corridor with me in Rome and gave me his blessing just before he slipped away to be with the Lord.

My breviary is crammed with many such photographs —not only of the dead but also of living friends and relatives who are scattered across the face of the earth. Abigail looks bright and ready to go at the age of two; my only godchild, Alexandra, is playing on a swing in New Jersey; there is David greeting me after his ordination in Birmingham. A 1981 card recalls a St. Patrick's Day meal out on the Via Appia with three friends who now live and work in Brazil, Canada and England.

The distant, as well as the dead, help to make up the communion of saints. The letters of St. Paul bear eloquent witness to the way this real union in Christ took (and can

148

continue to take) the sting out of the tyranny of distance. In the first century, travel was always tiring and often dangerous. But by writing to his scattered communities, the apostle encouraged and experienced himself the deep joy of their solidarity in Christ. His second letter to the Corinthians, the closest thing to an autobiography that Paul ever wrote, listed the great sufferings and deadly threats he continued to face. Nevertheless, he began by testifying to the rich consolation from God that he shared with his Christian friends in Greece. Nine times in just five verses he uses the noun and verb for "comfort" or "consolation" (2 Cor 1:3-7). Those verses also refer repeatedly to the apostle's sufferings and distress. But it is the sense of consolation that prevails.

Over the centuries Christians have known the same kind of comfort through remembering and communicating with other believers in various parts of the world. Few articles of the Creed have resonated more with their experience and practice. St. Paul was only the first in a long line of Christians whose letters witness to the way they have communicated light and life to each other—at a distance and sometimes at a considerable distance. I think here of writers like St. Teresa of Avila (1515-82), John Henry Newman (1801-90) and Dietrich Bonhoeffer (1906-45). Of course, these are big names to play with. Nevertheless, their letters to relatives, friends and other brothers and sisters in Christ reveal and reflect brilliantly those deep links in the communion of saints for which millions of others could vouch in their own simpler way.

Among the minor witnesses to the communion of saints, one of my favorites is a nineteenth century English clergyman, John Ellerton (1826-93). At night prayer we can still sing his hymn "The Day Thou Gavest, Lord, Is Ended." This hymn rejoices at the way in which Christians of the west take up God's praise as we retire for the night:

We thank Thee that thy Church unsleeping
While earth rolls onward into light,
Through all the world her watch is keeping,
And rests not now by day or night.

As over continent and island
The dawn leads on another day,
The voice of prayer is never silent,
Nor dies the strain of praise away.

The sun that bids us rest is waking
Our brethren 'neath the western sky,
And hour by hour fresh lips are making
Thy wondrous doings heard on high.

As regards the communion of saints there can be little difficulty about the dead and the distant. The brightness of memory reveals how God truly blessed the lives of our brothers and sisters "who have gone to their rest in the hope of rising again." It is easy to pray, "Bring them and all the departed into the light of your presence." Distance can likewise bring out the genuine holiness of the faithful who live in other cities, countries and continents. In this case distance lends truth, not false enchantment, to the view.

What is hardest perhaps is to acknowledge as a communion of saints the Christians who live with us and around us. It is their warts and faults that we notice too easily.

Nevertheless, if we let love guide our vision of these others, it will show us the truth. Despite their sinfulness, from baptism on God's good Spirit has been at work in their lives to sanctify them and prepare them for the full holiness of heaven. Love does not blind us to the truth but rather opens our eyes to make us sensitively aware of the presence of the Holy Spirit in Christians around us. Undoubtedly God has at times to write straight with crooked lines. But ultimately it is the goodness of God that writes the story of their lives and our lives. The Christians around us, no less than dead and distant Christians, make up the communion of saints.

In our first eucharistic prayer a roll-call of early Christian saints precedes and follows the consecration. The names ring out like beautiful bells: "Cornelius, Cyprian, Lawrence, Chrysogonus, Agnes, Cecilia, Anastasia." Those two lists are open-ended. They remind us of what all the baptized are and are called to be: saints shaped and guided here and now by the Holy Spirit to live forever in the final holiness of the hereafter.

In 1990 we celebrated one hundred years since the death of John Henry Newman. Among many other things, he left us a prayer that expresses beautifully the spiritual pilgrimage we all share in the communion of saints. Often used in the evening, this prayer points to the goal to which our spiritual union with Christ is leading us all.

O Lord, support us all the day long,
until the shadows lengthen and the evening comes,
and the busy world is hushed,
and the fever of life is over,
and our work is done.
Then in thy mercy grant us a safe lodging,
and a holy rest, and peace at the last.

While the Creed has been the subject of many paintings, to the best of my knowledge it has never been the theme of a great work of music. This is all the more surprising considering that its major structural divisions are very similar to those of a symphony. We have the majestic overture with God the creator, followed by the long second movement dedicated to God the Son. We then move into the lighter third movement, which begins with the Holy Spirit and ends with the forgiveness of sins,

151

before rising to the dramatic finale that reaches its climax with everlasting life. And just as the third movement in a symphony gives listeners a well earned respite from the complexities of what has preceded it, so here we are also given a moment to dream our ordinary dreams and come to terms with the ordinariness of our existence as human beings.

I often feel a pang of regret when saying the Nicene (rather than the Apostles') Creed that in this later statement of our belief there is no longer any specific mention of the communion of saints. It is rather as though all of us had been absorbed into the anonymity of the holy, catholic and apostolic church, stripped of our individual significance and identity.

The search for that fine balance between the whole and its parts is of course one of the recurring themes which dominate our lives. Too much emphasis on the individual may destroy the whole; too much interest in the whole may atrophy its working parts. From birth to death our attempt to find the perfect unity goes on.

As almost all of us are intimidated at one time or another by our very insignificance and transience, it is a comfort to be reminded as we are in the Apostles' Creed that our very ordinariness has a place in our Christian belief. Our belief is certainly about the divine but it is also about us.

Your chapter, Gerald, has centered on those men and women, famous or unknown, who have been of importance in your life. Each one of us has friendships and experiences similar to yours—they are unique but they are also part of our common inheritance as human beings. For me the communion of saints consists of all those fine threads of our common belief which link us to the people we have never known and will never meet, and of whose existence we are only dimly aware.

If you open a guide book to England, an ordinary rather than a very specialized one, you might read through to the end without discovering the names of the builders of the country's great cathedrals—Canterbury, Norwich, Salisbury, Wells, Winchester, York. Who were they? Do the same on a trip to Italy and you will have names spilling off the pages. Walk into any church anywhere in the country and you will be leafing through the lives of countless artists, architects, bishops, cardinals and popes. You may wander through a whole church without really seeing the church at all, so intent are you on the information in the book or the plaques along the walls. It takes courage to throw the book away. The temptation is to rush on to the next great work of art or the next great name. Here the little man—the cutter of the marble, the carver of the wooden garland, the molder of the brass, all of whom are vital to the final splendor of the whole creation—is forgotten beside the magnificence of the Giotto or the Pinturicchio.

It is easier to ponder the wonders of the nameless millions who have gone before us when surrounded by the simplicity of the northern Gothic. There, it is less difficult to feel at one with the unsung stone mason, the carpenter of the altar screen, the fashioner of the fan vaulting. Were they young or old, married or single? How did they live and die? What were their joys and passions? We shall never know, but what we do know, and perhaps what they never imagined, is that their simple, unchronicled labor still inspires our faith today.

Note. A few composers like Cherubini, Stravinsky and Vivaldi have set the Creed to music. However, these settings of the Creed are not among their most famous works. Furthermore, because of its length the Creed is often omitted in many great settings of the mass.

17

"The Forgiveness of Sins"

L uke's gospel ends with the promise that by witnessing to the risen Christ, the church will share
with all people the grace of repentance and the forgiveness of sins (Lk 24:27). Right from the day of Pentecost we
find Peter and the other apostles bringing the forgiveness
of sins through baptism and the gift of the Holy Spirit (Acts
2:37–42).

In the sacrament of penance the new formula of absolution speaks of the Holy Spirit "sent among us for the
forgiveness of sins." Beyond question, Luke would like
this change. Right from the beginning of his gospel he
presents the gift of salvation at least partly in terms of the
forgiveness of sins (Lk 1:77)—a theme to which Luke returns later in the gospel and in his second work, the Acts of
the Apostles.

If Luke highlights repentance and the forgiveness of
sins, he also illustrates what they mean by reporting Jesus'
parable of the prodigal son, a figure who is more accurately described as *the lost son* (Lk 15:11–32). Being
"lost" and then "found" is the profound way this parable
twice sums up the story of human repentance and divine
forgiveness (Lk 15:24, 32). Let this parable provide the
commentary on the Creed's phrase about "the forgiveness
of sins."

One of the commonest and most frightening human
experiences is the experience of loss. We may lose our

friends. We will lose opportunities. We must lose our health. We can lose our sense of direction, that clear recognition of what our Christian task is. We steadily suffer the loss of time, and we lose one thing on every occasion that we choose something else.

In *Burnt Norton*, T.S. Eliot wrote:

Footfalls echo in the memory
Down the passage which we did not take
Toward the door we never opened
Into the rose-garden.

How much did we lose by not taking that passage, by never opening that door, by not walking into that rose-garden? Memory can hurt and even torture us by recalling all that we have lost.

In Luke's gospel we find three parables about *loss* joined together in chapter 15: the parables of the lost sheep and the lost coin, and then the parable of the lost son. The first two parables deal with people who *search* for something they have lost: the shepherd hunting for the one sheep which has strayed away from the other ninety-nine, and the woman ransacking her dimly-lit hut until she finds the one coin that has fallen out of the purse in which she keeps her ten silver pieces. Those two stories are not concerned with the fact that the woman after she has suffered her loss still has ninety percent of her wealth and the shepherd still has ninety-nine percent of his flock. The stories seek to evoke a sense of the loss itself—the pain which the disappearance of money or livestock can cause.

Of course, the losses are slight: ten percent of the woman's cash and only one percent of the shepherd's flock. Yet such small losses can prove painful and frustrating. The recovery can be ever more joyful, encouraging and heartening than making the ten silver pieces or raising the hundred sheep was in the first place.

Jesus tells his stories to evoke that common feeling.

He does this in order to provide some insight into God's merciful attitude toward sinful men and women. God is glad to welcome back the godless, the irreligious, the sinner. There is joy in heaven even over one sinful person who repents.

In those two parables of the lost sheep and the lost coin we read of lost *property*. The next parable deals with the loss of *person*, a lost son. Unlike the preceding parables this parable has something to say about what happens to the one who is lost. The other two parables mention, of course, repentance: "There will be more joy in heaven over one sinful person who repents, than over ninety-nine upright people who do not need any repentance." The stories of the strayed sheep and the missing coin make this brief reference to repentance, but leave it unexplained. The parable of the prodigal son aims at offering some account of repentance.

It is the story of a farmer's younger son who is anxious about his freedom. He wants independence, the power to break with tradition, to get away and make his own decisions. Life at home becomes burdensome to him. He secures some property from his father, converts it into hard cash and heads off for a far country. Prostitutes and high living eat up the money. The boy is caught penniless when an economic crisis hits the country. Instead of doing what a practicing Jew should do—namely, look for the nearest Jewish community where he could find help and work— the prodigal son attaches himself to a Gentile farmer. He is sent out into the fields to work as a swineherd. For a good Jew there could hardly be any greater humiliation. Swine are unclean. To act as swineherd means incessant contact with these impure animals. The boy has effectively denied his religion; the sinner who began with prostitutes ends by becoming an apostate.

For his work he receives far too little food; he would love to eat some of the pods fed to the pigs. But he counts for less than the animals and is not allowed to take some of the pig-food for himself. In his hunger and humiliation he comes to himself, and decides to turn back to his father and to his God. He remembers what he has lost. He will return home and say to his father: "Father, I have sinned against heaven and in your eyes."

As the boy approaches home, his father sees him coming, forgets his dignity and runs out to greet him. Up to that point in the story the father has said *nothing—not a single word.* Now he begins to speak. He cuts short his son's apologies. He is not anxious to discuss matters, let alone impose conditions under which he is willing to receive his son back into the household. The father does not even make some declaration of pardon. Forgiveness is expressed by what he does. The boy receives the robe given to an honored guest. He is handed a ring to wear—presumably as a sign of his right to act again as a son. He is no longer allowed to go barefoot like a common laborer, but he wears the shoes that the free son of a free farmer should wear. The lost son who has come home is taken into the home for a feast of joy.

The party is well under way before the elder brother comes back from the fields, that elder son who has stayed loyally with his family and given his father service day-in and day-out. The father comes and begs him to join the party. In a very touching way the father pleads with him: "My dear child, what do you lose through my kindness? How am I doing you an injustice by celebrating the return of my lost son?" And there the parable ends—a challenge to its hearers in the time of Jesus and its readers now.

There is much in this parable of the lost son which speaks to the questions of choice, sin and repentance. The parable says something about that intriguing and fateful matter of *decision making.* Our lives, the lives of other people and the literature we read constantly confront us with that mysterious process by which men and women make major decisions about themselves, other people and God. Why—in T.S. Eliot's terms—did we decide not to

157

take that passage, never to open that door and never to go out into the rose-garden? At the climax of Iris Murdoch's novel *The Sandcastle,* why does the hero decide to remain seated at the dinner table, instead of rushing out after the girl with whom he has fallen in love? What happens when people take this kind of decision that can remake their lives either for evil or for good?

The prodigal son *comes to himself.* He is in a far country, caught in a situation of hunger and humiliation. But before he can find a way out of his appalling situation, he must first come to himself. He has run away from so much —including himself. If you like, he now emerges from his self-alienation. He finds himself. No one is there *to tell him* to make his decision or to urge him to adopt any particular course of action. All alone he decides. He must find himself before he will find his way out of his misery and back to his family.

Now think of the role played in the story by the other brother. A fairly grim sort of young man, he may be the elder of the two boys, but that does not stop him from behaving in an adolescent fashion. He sulks outside. When his father comes to plead with him, he refers to his brother not as "my brother," but as "this son of yours." It is an insolent, hateful phrase. If the younger son needs to repent, the elder brother must learn the lesson of love. A cold, unloving, self-righteous sort of person, at heart he is not a bit better than the fellow who took his money and went away. To the elder brother are spoken those lovely words: "My child, you have been with me always, and everything I have is yours." The father's meaning is clear: "You have missed the whole point. Why haven't you been happy? Why can't you love and joyfully welcome home your brother? Why have you turned to jealousy and bitterness?"

In each of us there can be something both of the younger son and of the elder brother. We may have strayed away from our Father's home—spiritually, mentally and emotionally. We may have chosen to live our lives elsewhere—in a far country, emotionally estranged from our Father. Or we may have always stayed with our Father but without really enjoying our life with him. We may have done our duty, and done it in a cold, unloving self-righteous way.

But we can always come to ourselves. No matter what our losses have been, we can always repent and return. We can always go in and enjoy our Father's home. We can always rest secure in the thought that he is always with us, and everything he has is ours.

The parable of the prodigal son turns up in chapter 15 of Luke. A little later in the same gospel we find the purpose of the parable expressed through the story of a sinner whom Jesus went out of his way to seek and save (Lk 19:1–10). In the parable it is the prodigal son himself who returns home. In the story of the sinful and repentant publican it is Jesus himself who goes to the house of Zacchaeus. Either way the point for us is the same: through Jesus and the gift of the Holy Spirit our God wishes to deliver us from sin, bring us to repentance and give us the joy of being radically forgiven.

Both in the parable and in the Zacchaeus story one word we might have expected is never used explicitly: love. Nevertheless, both texts speak eloquently of our merciful God who says to us: "I love every one of you too much to let any of you be lost. I want each one of you to be with me and live a life of joy beyond your wildest dreams."

"**D**o you still love me?" was a question the children would sometimes ask when still young after they had been particularly naughty. It seemed difficult for them to understand that, however cross I may have been, my love for them didn't change. In their eyes anger appeared to exclude the possibility of love.

Perhaps the feelings of the one who loves are always something of a mystery to the one who is loved. Did the prodigal son ever really understand the pain or the joy that he caused his father? The story itself would indicate that he did not. He clearly never expected that his return, motivated by his own hunger and not by love of his father, would have caused such a spontaneous, all-loving reaction.

In more reflective moments I sometimes feel that this parable has the wrong name. Wouldn't it have been more appropriate to call it the parable of the loving father rather than the prodigal son? So intent are we on interpreting the misdeeds of the younger son and his jealous brother that we often overlook the feelings of the father. It is very easy for us to identify either with the seemingly unjust treatment allotted to the older brother, or with the despair and then the trepidation which the younger must have felt on his journey home. It takes another dimension—the understanding of love rather than the knowledge of sin—to find ourselves in the role of the father of the tale.

There are no limits to the love the father feels for his son. His is an infinite process of giving to his child. His gift of love is twofold. It contains first and foremost the gift of freedom, followed subsequently by that of forgiveness. Both are unconditional. The price of the first is pain: that of the second, immense joy.

In the parable the father puts no constraints on his son as he leaves home. There is no effort to hold him back. On the contrary the father gives his child all that he is due; he gives him the most and the best that he can before the boy sets out down the road he has chosen. There are no conditions such as, "Yes, you may go, but . . ." What parent does not feel this anguish as a child leaves home? But what human parent does not hedge the departure with conditions, with attempts to circumscribe in some way—perhaps emotionally or financially—the freedom of the child to choose his or her own future? It takes the ultimate in

160

love to give total freedom to another, fully aware of the pain this will cause the parent and maybe even the child.

The child, intent on his own desires, oblivious of his parent's pain, disappears without trace. The father has given up the one he loves in giving freedom, even the freedom to choose what is wrong. The father makes no demands on this freedom. He doesn't follow his son, doesn't try to persuade him to come home, doesn't beg him to think about the state of the family left behind, never reminds him of his obligations and responsibilities, never mentions his own sorrow. He waits, silently. Then without warning his son comes home. The joy, like the previous gift of freedom, is unconditional. No questions asked, no searching for motives, no reproaches. The child is back and that is enough.

The forgiveness is total. The child, prepared to accept the least the father might offer, is given the most and is reinstated in his former place. For the father, at least, the years in the wilderness make no difference to the love for his son, and in the giving of the love there is now great joy. Perhaps the words of St. Paul to the Corinthians, which I have already used in Chapter 9 but make no apologies for quoting again here at greater length, can best describe the love of the father for the prodigal son:

> Love is patient and kind: love is not jealous or boastful; it is not arrogant or rude. Love does not insist on its own way; it is not irritable or resentful; it does not rejoice at wrong, but rejoices in the right. Love bears all things, believes all things, hopes all things, endures all things. Love never ends.

If I were allowed to add one thing to St. Paul's wonderful definition of love, it would surely be: "Love forgives all things."

18

"The Resurrection of the Body"

"**H**ow are the dead raised? With what kind of body do they come?" (1 Cor 15:35). At the climax of his first letter to the Corinthians St. Paul wrestles with these questions. Christ's victory over death anticipated and initiated the resurrection of all the dead. It was, so to speak, "the first fruits" of that general harvest (1 Cor 15:20). But can we understand and explain how human beings and their world will be raised up and transformed when the new heaven and the new earth come (Rev 21:1; 2 Pet 3:13; Rom 8:18–23)?

At first glance it would seem much easier if Christians were to join Plato and others in holding a straightforward immortality of the soul and dropped all hope for a resurrection of the body. In that vision of death our imperishable soul escapes from the prison of the body to live on forever in the real, spiritual world, leaving behind the laws and theories of our physical existence.

In Chapter 4 we saw how the laws and findings of the new physics and, in particular, the theory of the Big Bang lend a certain plausibility to belief in an intelligent creator and designer who purposefully organized the universe and its finely tuned laws to bring about the emergence of human life. Modern physics may make it easier to accept God as "creator of heaven and earth." But, as the last act in our story, scientists expect the sun to burn out and all life to end on our planet. This casts doubt on any hope for bodily resurrection in a transformed world. In brief, while lending some support to what the Creed has to say about our origins, contemporary physics offers a gloomy picture about the final future of our universe or at least our little corner of it. Did we come from the Big Bang only to end with the Big Burnout?

Problems with modern physics, however, cannot excuse attempts to spiritualize our version of resurrection to the point that it becomes indistinguishable from the mere survival of immortal souls in a world that has nothing to do with our own. Being human means being essentially bodily and social. Our bodiliness relates us to other people in the narrower community of our families and the wider community of the whole human race. Without our bodies we would not even come into existence, let alone live our human lives in society. Through our bodies we are also related to the widest community of all, nature and the whole created cosmos, exchanging matter with our environment at the rate of millions of cells each day.

Our body has put us into a lifelong relationship with other human beings and the world. It is in our bodiliness that we will be raised to a new and definitive life.

As regards the Big Bang, we have no access to the situation "before" it. We do not see its cause at work (the creator) but only its effects (the universe). As regards the Big Burnout, we see what will be affected by it (we ourselves and our environment) but not yet its aftermath (a resurrected humanity and world). We cannot describe either the "before" (the situation "prior" to the creation) or the "after" (the future world) in the way we can describe this world and what we find in it.

Nevertheless, our faith in God as creator encourages us to hope for what God promises to bring about in the new creation (a definitive life for a resurrected humanity and a resurrected world). The greater our wonder at God's extraordinary act in creating the enormous universe out of nothing and maintaining it constantly in existence, the ore we will be ready to cherish our hope for the resurrection of human beings and their world. Faith in God as creator and as resurrector go hand in hand.

In creation God brought into existence what had not yet existed. "Before" creation there was nothing. In the new creation of resurrection God will bring "back" to a transformed life what had once existed and now has suffered the radical breakdown of death. In a sense resurrection is a more manageable notion for us. Unlike creation (which involves a passage from nothing to something), resurrection involves a passage from something (through death) to a new and greater something.

In parenthesis let me note why it was necessary in the last three paragraphs to surround "before," "prior" and "after" with quotation marks. Time and temporal relations of before and after exist only in reference to the physical world. Properly (= temporally) speaking, one cannot ask about the situation before the universe existed or after it ends. That would be like asking about something north of the North Pole or south of the South Pole. As regards the creation and disappearance of the physical universe as we know it, the "before" and "after," respectively, are only logical distinctions.

Last year I gave a lecture on the resurrection at the University of Christchurch in New Zealand. The first person to ask a question put his chief difficulty this way: "What do you mean by the *transformation* involved in resurrection?" Perhaps without realizing it, he was in effect repeating Paul's questions: "How are the dead raised? With what kind of body do they come?"

In this chapter and earlier in this book (dealing with God as creator) I have attempted to enter into some dialogue with modern science. Here I want to seek help from art and contemplation to offer some response to the question: What will our transformed, risen existence be like?

First of all, painters and sculptors can entice us to reflect on the risen life more imaginatively, creating fresh

164

symbols through which we might anticipate a new experience. In dealing with the human body, artists as different as El Greco and Rodin discover and set free a kind of second body. They go behind the familiar appearance of the human body to reexpress it in a new way. From the organic, material bodies in front of them, they disengage not mere replicas in which we can discern a likeness, but hidden things of splendor and beauty. They discover an inner glory in their subjects and, as it were, transcribe them into another world. The creative intuitions and hands of the artists liberate a new life within ordinary life. Art, in short, sublimates the dull-looking reality of human bodies.

St. Paul repeatedly speaks of God the Father as having raised Jesus from the dead (e.g. Gal 1:1; 1 Thes 1:9–10; Rom 10:9). He cautions the Corinthians against fornication by recalling their bodily destiny: "God raised the Lord and will also raise us up by his power" (1 Cor 6:14). Dare we represent God the Father as the supreme artist who has discovered and set free Jesus' final bodily glory and will do the same for us? In sublimating in this way his crucified Son, he promises to transcribe us into the splendor and beauty of what Paul calls the "spiritual body" (1 Cor 15:44). Some minds at least can move with natural ease from the lesser wonder of artistic creation to the greater wonder of God's new creation. The resurrection can be seen as nothing less than the divine artist disengaging our hidden body of glory.

Paul encourages such an imaginative leap from the lesser to the greater when he introduces an analogy from his Jewish background. Even dull readers, he expects, can marvel at the growth from grain to harvest:

> Someone will ask, how are the dead raised? With what kind of body do they come? You foolish man! What you sow does not come to life unless it dies. And what you sow is not the body which is to be, but a bare kernel, perhaps of wheat or of some other grain. But

God gives it a body he has chosen, and to each kind of
seed its own body (1 Cor 15:35–38).

Here Paul invites his readers, for all their foolishness,
to make the leap from the lesser miracle of harvest to the
greater wonder of the risen life.

So it is with the resurrection of the dead. What is sown
is perishable, what is raised is imperishable. It is sown
in weakness, it is raised in power. It is sown a physical
body, it is raised a spiritual body (1 Cor 15:42–44).

In his preaching, Jesus never observes, "The spiritual,
risen body will be like unto . . ." Nevertheless, his parables and, in general, his teaching anticipate the route of
the Pauline imagination in 1 Corinthians—a movement
from the lesser to the greater. Marriage feasts symbolize
the big party God will throw at the end of time. Travelers
turning up late at night and looking for food suggest the
nature of persistent prayer to God. A father's loving welcome to a renegade son serves to picture the divine mercy.
Sunshine and rain reflect God's free generosity to all alike.
Over and over again Jesus asks his listeners to let the ordinary things and events around them become the means for
understanding and accepting God's activity on their
behalf.

Of course, our modern knowledge of botany and agriculture can get in the way of entering enthusiastically into
Paul's particular example. Genetics, fertilizers and trac-
tors have sapped the wonders of the harvest. All the same,
we can substitute other examples and imitate Jesus and
Paul in jumping from the ordinary or extraordinary things
of human experience to the objects of our faith and hope.
In particular, the ways that great artists render the human
body can make some sense of what risen existence could
be like.

Reflection on genuine contemplative, ascetics and mystics may also yield a hard nugget of imaginative truth about resurrection life. True contemplatives and ascetics give up or at least curtail a number of normal human activities. They substitute hours of prayer for other occupations. They may sleep less than others. They often engage in fasting. Many renounce marriage. Some stay in one place. All in all, they abandon much that seems to make human existence worthwhile. Yet far from living less than others, they appear in some ways to live more. Their asceticism looks like a putting to death. But at least in the case of genuine ascetics and contemplatives this apparent "mortification" is really a "vivification." Remarkable powers of energy and insight are released. Pain and fear lose their grip. A new freedom arises to overcome the limitations of ordinary lives. The mind and will function in ways that go beyond what men and women normally experience.

Like countless contemplatives, ascetics and mystics, Jesus passed by much that seems to make human life valuable. He never married, confined his active career to a couple of years spent in a pocket-handkerchief country, and cut sleep short to spend hours in prayer while the world which he challenged to repent rapidly turned dangerous. In many ways Jesus came across as someone who lived less than others—that "son of man" who had "nowhere to lay his head" (Mt 8:20). Yet he was remembered as the one empowered to heal others (Mk 5:30). Even if the gospels never described his physical appearance, nevertheless they recalled one occasion during his ministry when bright glory shone through Jesus:

> And after six days Jesus took with him Peter, James and John, and led them up a high mountain apart by themselves; and he was transfigured before them, and his garments became glistening, intensely white, as no fuller on earth could bleach them (Mk 9:2–3).

Such luminous and powerful moments from the story of Jesus and of some of his saintly followers offer memorable glimpses of what resurrection life could be like. These occasions form living parables when the gap between the here and the hereafter closes a little and we can say, "The resurrection will be like unto the moment when . . ."

To conclude. The terminology of Teilhard de Chardin provides another avenue for approaching the resurrection and its result, the spiritual body or a human, bodily existence completely guided by God's Spirit. The mutation from the biosphere to the noosphere is an image of the greater mutation from the noosphere to what can be called the pneumatosphere or realm of the Spirit. The first mutation brought the appearance of thought. Human thought can embrace the universe. It can reach out instantly across millions of miles of space or back through endless centuries of time. But human activity fails to keep pace with thought. Our actions remain pinned down and engulfed by the universe. The transformation which came with the appearance of thought has not yet occurred for human activity. Can we imagine resurrection as a mutation from the noosphere to the pneumatosphere, such as will bring for human action the kind of metamorphosis which has already taken place for human thought?

In our next chapter we will comment on "life everlasting," a deeply consoling article of the Creed that also implies a note of somber warning.

In all the previous chapters we have in some way or another pinned our belief to our personal experience. Daily life has in many ways helped enlighten even the most difficult parts of the Creed. But here in these last two articles of our belief we are cut loose and forced to speculate.

Even the gospels, full of help and guidance on how we should lead our earthly lives, give us frustratingly little on what we can expect ahead. We are left to imagine and wonder.

Our leap into the unknown is inevitably conditioned by our own human limitations. We are tied by earthly concepts and our own physical conditions and environment. It is all very fine to talk of the resurrection of the body when we are healthy and young. But it is possible to imagine countless cases in which the human body is nothing but a living prison. In these cases thoughts of carrying it and what it has made of our lives over into an after-life may seem like an intolerable nightmare. An imprisoned sufferer might well pray to be freed forever of all traces and reminders of a previous earthly existence.

The hope for the resurrection of the body is therefore in a very real way conditioned by our earthly experience. Furthermore the images we use to convey our hopes are strictly curtailed by a language which we use to communicate common events and occurrences. How is it possible to describe extraordinary happenings in ordinary terms?

Specialized subjects now use ever more specialized language to convey their meaning. Long-gone are the days when a theologian might have applied himself to astronomy or a physician to philosophy. Sociology, economics, nuclear physics, bio-chemistry, informatics and even agriculture all use their own highly technical language to convey their meaning, much to the despair of newcomers to the field. Gerald, you mention Teilhard de Chardin, a man who felt that his new concepts needed new words. You yourself point above to the inappropriateness of using simple concepts such as "before" and "after" to convey your meaning in particular passages.

I would go further and argue that in this chapter one of our greatest difficulties is with our understanding of the meaning of the word "body" itself, just as in the next chapter we have to struggle with two no less complex and seemingly contradictory words, "life" and "everlasting." But if we are unable to define these words satisfactorily in

169

common language, then our faith threatens to become unconvincing just when it is put to its hardest test.

The word "body" when we talk in terms of resurrection invariably conjures up visions of our physical being, the biological entity with which we are blessed or cursed, or as *Webster's Dictionary* defines it: "the material part or nature of a human being."

If we stick to our purely physical bodies when contemplating the resurrection, we run up against the difficulties which plagued our ancestors for centuries. But if we jettison the physical in favor of some disembodied spirit or soul, we run into the difficulties which we have already discussed in Chapter 11.

Let us therefore take two other definitions to be found in *Webster's* of the word "body": "a mass of matter distinct from other masses," or again: "the main part of a literary or journalistic work." Here we have two ideas for the one concept: something which distinguishes one thing from another, and a unity or a whole.

It is in fact our bodies which separate one individual from another. But they also unite us to each other and to Christ in our commonly shared human experience. Husband and wife are separate beings, but in their moments of closest physical love they unite. Before their bodies break apart once more, they may have set in motion that miraculous sequence of creation in which two separate cells fuse, lose their individual identity and form a new, separate whole which, regardless of its microscopic size, contains all those genetic messages which are vital for the start of another human life.

Our bodies are in fact endless sources of contradiction. They are totally vulnerable but amazingly strong. They resist great strain but succumb to devastating destruction in an instant. They are the cause of great suffering but also of intense joy. A voice raised in anger may quickly be replaced by a loving kiss.

Our bodies can be the inspiration for our greatest

achievements or they can frustrate our noblest aspirations. They dazzle us with the greatness of their beauty or they torture us with sights of nauseating decay. When young and healthy we would cling to them forever. When suffering or old they become unforgiving prisons caging those longing to break free. They are transitory combinations of liquids, gases and minerals, never randomly associated, but forever changing.

As a child I loved looking down the cone of a kaleidoscope, that old fashioned toy now almost impossible to find. If you twisted it one way you would see a certain colorful pattern; twist it again and other shapes would appear. The glass elements at the end of the tube were always the same but the patterns were always different. To get the full effect of those ever changing combinations and colors you had to hold the kaleidoscope up to the light.

Our bodies today are far removed from what they were at birth. They are probably considerably different from what they will be at death. But the elements are still the same now as they were at the moment of our conception. Should we therefore marvel that when we are held up to the fullness of the divine light, even more spectacular colors and combinations will be revealed?

19

"And Life Everlasting"

Eternal life means heaven, whereas hell is "eternal punishment" (Mt 25:46). Heaven will bring a perfect communion with God which the New Testament sometimes pictures and sometimes leaves quite obscure. "Eye has not seen nor ear heard, nor has the human heart conceived what God has prepared for those who love him" (1 Cor 2:9). Hell means a final separation from God brought about through one's own fault. St. Paul and other New Testament witnesses name sinful actions and omissions that could exclude one from the kingdom of God (Mt 25:31–46; 1 Cor 6:9–10; Gal 5:20–21; Eph 5:5; Rev 21:8).

As I pointed out in Chapter 13, sinful alienation from other human beings and God *could* reach the point of bringing eternal damnation. Human malice and the deliberate misuse of freedom *could* put one in hell. We simply do not know whether this has happened or will happen to any men or women. But the possibility remains as an awesome warning about where freely chosen evil could take us. At the same time we can pray that God will be "everything to everyone" (1 Cor 15:28), in the sense that all people will be finally saved.

Heaven means seeing God, no longer as mirrored dimly in the world we know, but face to face (1 Cor 13:12). The God whom we will experience most fully is tripersonal. Hence we can speak of heaven as being raised

172

by the Spirit to be completely with Christ and through him with the Father.

Artists have taken their cue from the Bible to depict heaven as a garden of paradise or a heavenly city. There the community of the blessed, in a face to face situation (1 Jn 3:2), will know God as the end and goal of all their desires. For those who love gardens and cities, the images of the perfect garden and the most beautiful city (Rev 21:1–22:19) can prompt useful intuitions. But what of the heart of heavenly life, our utterly fulfilling vision of the Trinity?

At times the scriptures present negatively the central reality of heaven. Death, pain and injustice will no longer afflict us (Rev 21:4). Positively speaking, God will be with us (Rev 21:3) to fulfill utterly the deepest desires of our hearts. We hunger and thirst for the fullness of life, total truth and never-ending love. In God we will find all that, far beyond the partial life, fragmentary meaning and imperfect love we now experience.

Some books of the New Testament present heaven as a marriage feast that never ends. Over the centuries a number of Christian writers have taken off from that image and trivialized heaven as little more than a home for reunited lovers. Beyond question, the meeting again theme can be justified. But heaven will be primarily a meeting again with Christ who promises: "When I go and prepare a place for you, I will come again and take you to myself, that where I am you also may be" (Jn 14:3). We will meet again our families and friends. But by themselves, neither here nor hereafter, can they give us a supremely satisfying existence. The primary source of our everlasting happiness will be the tripersonal God made known to us through Jesus Christ.

As in the case of the risen body, we cannot describe eternal life in the way that we can describe objects in this world. Our final existence with God is the object of our religious hope and not a theme of scientific knowledge.

Nevertheless, images and analogies drawn from science and elsewhere can help us at least a little to understand eternal life. Take the incredible size and power of our universe, a result coming from the first instant of the Big Bang when there was zero mass and infinite density.

Fifteen billion years later, to cross our galaxy (the Milky Way) it would take us 100,000 years traveling at the speed of light. Astronomers estimate that there are at least a hundred billion other galaxies beyond the Milky Way. The ordered cosmos points to a God of astonishing power and wisdom. Those divine attributes mirrored in the universe which we see can make it easier to believe that we will find God's goodness and beauty to be also astonishingly great and supremely satisfying.

Perhaps the fear of boredom still lurks around and makes heaven less than fully desirable. On the one hand, we now experience how transient all things are. No moment, even the best and the happiest, ever remains. But, on the other hand, when our eternity begins, will it be a never-ending way of existing that threatens to be infinitely long and boring? The truth is rather that eternal life, instead of being an existence that just goes on and on, means rather existing "simultaneously." In an eternal now God will get everything together for us. We will be freed from the tyranny of time to share, as far as that is possible, in the "simultaneous" existence of eternity.

Here, perhaps more than anywhere else, the language of the liturgy can engage us and lead us to the truth. Let me give the last word to the preface from a mass for the dead.

In Christ who rose from the dead our hope of resurrection dawned. The sadness of death gives way to the bright promise of immortality. Lord, for your faithful people life is changed, not ended. When the body of our earthly dwelling lies in death we gain an everlasting dwelling place in heaven.

174

Here in the last chapter we come face to face with the tensions inherent in the phrase "life everlasting." It is as though all those conflicts at the heart of the human person which we examined in chapter 1 are summed up in these two words. Here we have the finite and the infinite, the transient and the eternal, the human and the divine.

Who has not looked up at the sky on a bright, starlit night and felt the terror of one's own insignificance beside that immeasurable expanse of dark blue? But who has not also felt the exact opposite—sheer overwhelming thanks for the infinity above? Who has not turned in comfort to the eternal present of the "I am" in the book of Revelation: " 'I am the Alpha and the Omega,' says the Lord, who is and who was and who is to come, the Almighty" (Rev 1:8).

Being finite human beings, infinity is difficult or nearly impossible to grasp. *"Nulla si sa; tutto si immagina,"* said a character in *Voce della Luna*, one of the more poetic films of Federico Fellini. How little we know about life everlasting and how much we imagine! We imagine everything and the reverse of everything in our visions of heaven and hell. Every one of our five senses has been brought into play to conjure up visions of the hereafter. Art, music, drama, dance, literature and cinema have attempted to find the key to the life ahead.

Interpretations offered by one generation do not necessarily satisfy another. We pick and choose what suits us best. But if we are honest, we are forced to admit that all we know is that we really don't know at all. And it is as we admit the limitations of our human knowledge that we stand each Sunday, or perhaps each day, and say together in faith and trust and hope: "We believe."

20

"Amen"

This book on the Apostles' Creed has shared the meaning and truth which Mary and I find in this summary of Christian beliefs. May all our readers join us in saying "Amen" to these basic propositions of faith.

Those who wish more information and insight might find help in the bibliography that follows. They can also learn much from Christian liturgy, popular devotion and art which express in life the articles of faith listed by the Creed.

Finally, a word of advice for those fortunate enough to visit Italy. You would do well to stop in Siena and see the chapel in its city hall. On the choir stalls a fifteenth century artist, Domenico Spinelli di Niccolò, has left twenty-two wooden inlays to illustrate the articles of the Nicene Creed. The last of these magnificent pieces of mosaic woodwork represents eternal life as angels in worship playing musical instruments before the Father, Son and Holy Spirit.

If you love music, you may well share Spinelli's image of heaven as a sacred concert that will never end. That, after all, is the way the book of Psalms closes. The last psalm runs through the instruments of an ancient orchestra to tell everyone and everything, "Praise the Lord."

Suggestions for Further Reading

J.-N. Bezançon et al., *How To Understand the Creed* (London, 1987).

D.B. Bryan, *From Bible to Creed* (Wilmington, 1988).

F.L. Cross and E.A. Livingstone (eds.), *The Oxford Dictionary of the Christian Church* (2nd ed., London, 1974).

G.J. Dyer (ed.), *An American Catholic Catechism* (New York, 1975).

The German Bishops' Conference, *The Church's Confession of Faith* (San Francisco, 1987).

J.N.D. Kelly, *Early Christian Creeds* (3rd ed., New York, 1972).

J.A. Komonchak et al. (eds.), *The New Dictionary of Theology* (Wilmington, 1987).

B.L. Marthaler, *The Creed* (Mystic, 1987).

R.P. McBrien, *Catholicism* (study ed., San Francisco, 1986).

New Catholic Encyclopedia, 15 vols (New York, 1967), supplementary vols. 1974, 1976 and 1989.

P. Perkins, *What We Believe: A Biblical Catechism of the Apostles' Creed* (Mahwah, 1986).

J. Ratzinger, *Introduction to Christianity* (New York, 1970).

A. Richardson and J. Bowden (eds.), *The Westminster Dictionary of Christian Theology* (Philadelphia, 1983).

The Apostles' Creed

I believe in God, the Father almighty,
*   creator of heaven and earth*
I believe in Jesus Christ, his only Son, our Lord.
*   He was conceived by the power of the Holy Spirit*
*   and born of the Virgin Mary.*
*   He suffered under Pontius Pilate,*
*   was crucified, died, and was buried.*
*   He descended to the dead.*
*   On the third day he rose again.*
*   He ascended into heaven,*
*   and is seated at the right hand of the Father.*
*   He will come again to judge the living and the dead.*
I believe in the Holy Spirit,
*   the holy catholic Church,*
*   the communion of saints,*
*   the forgiveness of sins,*
*   the resurrection of the body,*
*   and the life everlasting. Amen.*